HUMAN CAPITAL AND GROWTH

HUMAN CAPITAL AND GROWTH

PAULO S. TENANI

M. Books do Brasil Editora Ltda.

Av. Brigadeiro Faria Lima, 1993 - 5º andar - Cj. 51
01452-001 - São Paulo - SP Telefones: (11) 3168-8242/(11) 3168-9420
Fax: (11) 3079-3147 - e-mail: vendas.mbooks@terra.com.br

Cataloging-in-Publication Data

Tenani, Paulo Sérgio

   Human Capital and Growth / Paulo Sérgio Tenani

   Includes index
   ISBN 85-89384-16-0
   1. Economy.   2. Finance.

Copyright © 2004 by Paulo Sérgio Tenani. All rights reserved. No part of this publication may be reproduced, stored or transmitted in any form without the prior written permission of the M. Books do Brasil Editora Ltda.

Publisher: Milton Mira de Assumpção Filho
Interior and Cover Design: ERJ

First printing

To Kelvin Lancaster and Werner Baer

ACKNOWLEDGMENTS

This research benefited from contributions by Roberto Apelfeld, Werner Baer, Jess Benhabib, Dan Biller, Duncan Foley, Kelvin Lancaster, Ron Miller, Pedro Paulo Schirmer and Xavier Sala-i-Martin. Roberto Apelfeld continuously reminded me to pay closer attention to the global picture rather than the details (as also did Duncan Foley). We discussed the research in many circumstances and his comments were essential for a better understanding of the model. Werner Baer stressed the importance of deriving economic intuition from the mathematical techniques, and has been an important influence in my development as an economist. Jess Benhabib suggested the topic, taught me a great deal of Growth Theory and indicated the basic model (without physical capital) that would clarify the reason why the speed of convergence of the two-sector growth model is independent of preference parameters. Benhabib's work with Roberto Perli, Aldo Rustichini and Mark Spiegel were the starting point of my research. Dan Biller read and commented all the chapters, and pointed out that there was no need to assume a CES instantaneous utility function to derive convergence properties. Duncan Foley suggested that the results I obtained for the Cobb-Douglas production technology would probably hold for more general linear homogeneous functions. His comments allowed me to greatly improve the research. Kelvin Lancaster pointed out that the first two rows of the characteristic matrix of the Mulligan and Sala-i-Martin three-dimensional system were linearly dependent, which led to the conclusion that, in the two-sector framework, the transitional dynamics was independent of utility parameters. Lancaster followed all the steps of the research, thus solving innumerous problems. Ron Miller was able to understand in five minute what took me weeks to realize. He pointed out new directions and, in many circumstances, provided the intuition needed to proceed with the research. Pedro Paulo Schirmer suggested the transformation that led to the interpretation of the dynamic budget constraint, the human capital accumulation condition and the dynamic Euler equation as comprising a three-dimensional linear non-autonomous system of differential equations. Xavier Sala-i-Martin taught me a great deal of Growth Theory and co-authored a wonderful book on the topic. His work on the two-sector model was a strong motivation for this book.

ABSTRACT

HUMAN CAPITAL AND GROWTH

Whenever the production functions for physical and human capital are homogeneous of the first degree, the non-linear differential system that governs the dynamics of the two-sector economy can actually be divided into a single non-linear differential equation, representing a tendency for returns to be equalized, and a linear three dimensional non-autonomous differential system, which stands for how consumption as well as physical and human capital adjust to this tendency. This interpretation of the dynamics allows for an easy derivation of stability and convergence properties, and gives a clear account for the single economic force driving the system towards its steady-state equilibrium, namely returns equalization.

FOREWORD

There is no more fascinating question in Economic Theory than the role of Human Capital formation in the process of Economic Growth. In fact, since the mid 1980's – after Robert Lucas´ and Paul Romer´s revival of Growth Theory – a great deal of economic literature has been dedicated to modeling human capital formation as one of the main determinants of long-term growth. However, the difficulties that arise from the complicated interaction between human and physical capital accumulation, led most of the authors to concentrate their analysis on the long-run properties of the model, relegating the short-term dynamics to a secondary role. Mr. Tenani´s work is an exception to this rule. In this short and fascinating book on "Human Capital and Growth", he is able to reduce what at first seemed to be a complicated problem into a surprisingly simpler one. More than developing an Endogenous Growth Model, Mr. Tenani sheds light on how a growing Economy evolves over time and develops an interesting framework to be used by all those researchers in the field.

                                        Roberto Luis Troster
                                        Chief Economist
                                        Federation of Brazilian Banks (FEBRABAN)
                                        Professor of Economics
                                        Pontifícia Universidade Católica

TABLE OF CONTENTS

Introduction .... **XV**

Chapter 1 – Human Capital and Growth **1**
    1.1 Introduction 3
    1.2 The model 5
        1.2.1 Consumers 5
            1.2.1.1 The first-order conditions 7
            1.2.1.2 Human capital accumulation 9
        1.2.2 Firms 11
        1.2.3 General equilibrium 12
    1.3 Transitional Dynamics 14
    1.4 Steady-state equilibrium 18
    1.5 Conclusion 23

Chapter 2 – On the Speedy of Convergence of Economic Growth Models **25**
    2.1 Introduction 27
    2.2 The speed of convergence in the neoclassical growth model 28
    2.3 The speed of convergence in the two-sector growth model 31
    2.4 Conclusion 35

Chapter 3 – A One-Dimensional Interpretation for the Transitional Dynamics of Two-Sector Models of Endogenous Growth **37**
    3.1 Introduction 39
    3.2 The standard two-sector growth model 39
    3.3 The three dimensional approach of Mulligan and Sala-i-Martin 41
    3.4 A one-dimensional interpretation 43
    3.5 Conclusion 46

Appendixes **47**
    Appendix 1 – The intertemporal allocation condition 49
    Appendix 2 – The non-autonomous system in k[t], h[t] and c[t] 50
    Appendix 3 – The Solow-Ramsey model 52
    Appendix 4 – The two-sector model 54
    Appendix 5 – The three dimensional system 61
    Appendix 6 – The linear non-autonomous system 63

References **64**

Index **65**

INTRODUCTION

This book presents a contribution to the analysis of the transitional and steady-state dynamics of the two-sector growth model, for the general case in which the production functions are homogeneous of the first degree and the instantaneous utility function is strictly concave.

Since the 1980's, after Robert Lucas (1988) and Paul Romer (1986) revival of the Theory of Economic Growth, a great deal of the economic literature has been dedicated to modeling human capital formation as one of the main determinants of long-term growth. The difficulties that arise from the complicated interaction between human and physical capital accumulation, however, led most of the authors to focus their analysis on the steady-state properties of the model, relegating the transitional dynamics to a secondary role.

The exceptions to this rule were Mulligan and Sala-i-Martin (1993) and Caballé and Santos (1993), who tackled the problem and succeed in proving stability and convergence properties. Mulligan and Sala-i-Martin (1993), in particular, were able to reduce by one-dimension the complicated non-linear differential system that governed the evolution of the two-sector growth model, giving the first economic insight for the major forces that come into play during the transition.

This book is in the spirit of Mulligan and Sala-i-Martin, in the sense that it also simplifies the two-sector growth model in order to derive some economic intuition regarding its behavior. However, approaching the model from a different angle, I was able to show that what at first seemed to be a complicated non-linear differential system, could actually be interpreted as one single non-linear differential equation, representing a tendency for returns to be equalized, and a three dimensional linear but non-autonomous system, describing how consumption as well as physical and human capital adjust to this tendency.

Chapters 1, 2 and 3 present the different consequences of this idea. Chapter 1 investigates a general formulation of the two-sector growth model, in which the production of human capital is a function of real investment in formal instruction as well as human capital. By allowing for the fact that individuals have to finance their way through school, an additional factor to the education process is brought into the analysis, with important implications for both the transitional and steady-state dynamics of the system. During the transition, changes in real wages will no longer exclusively affect the opportunity cost of going to school, but will also influence the quality of the school attended by individuals. The net result will be such that the return to accumulating human capital converges to that of holding assets and vice-versa. The steady-state growth rate is the outcome of this process, being a function of parameters describing both the consumption and education sectors of the model. Chapter 2 shows that, if the production functions for physical and human capital are linear homogeneous functions, then the speed of convergence of the two-sector growth model is fully determined by technological parameters, being independent of the discount rate and the instantaneous utility function. Preference parameters, however, will have an important role in determining the steady-state growth rate of the model, a result that was already apparent from the analysis of Chapter 1. Finally, Chapter 3 deals with the relation between Mulligan and Sala-i-Martin (1993) analysis and the approach used in Chapters 1 and 2. It is shown that Mulligan and Sala-i-Martin (1993) research had already suggested that a further reduction of the dynamics of the two-sector model was possible, since the first two lines of the characteristic matrix of their three dimensional system were linearly dependent.

Chapter 1

Human Capital and Growth

Investment in schooling has important implications for both the steady-state and transitional dynamics of two sector-models of endogenous growth. If the agent has to pay his way through school, the marginal product of the human capital he allocates to studying will be higher whenever he can afford a better school. In general equilibrium this implies that the growth rate of the economy will be a function of both technological as well as human capital parameters.

1.1 Introduction

What is the role of human capital in the process of economic growth? This question, which was asked by Hirofumi Uzawa as early as 1961, has received renewed attention after Robert Lucas'1988 seminal work. Papers by Sergio Rebelo (1991), Casey Mulligan and Xavier Sala-i-Martin (1993), Jordi Caballé and Manuel Santos (1993) and Benhabib and Perli (1994) have expanded Lucas analysis in various directions, in addition to elaborating on the out-of-the-steady-state dynamic properties of his model. On the empirical side, the work by Mankiw, Romer and Weil (1992) and Benhabib and Spiegel (1994) have added to the discussion by trying to measure the total significance of human capital, as well as verifying the different channels through which it acts upon growth.

This chapter is a contribution to this on going literature. The question we ask is how the Lucas (1988) model would change if human capital were also a function of real investment in schooling. And our answer to this question is that it changes substantially. If the agent has to pay his way through school, the marginal product of the human capital he allocates to studying will be higher whenever he can afford a better school. Thus, one should expect, high real wages would imply more education and more human capital formation. This effect, however, is not present in the Lucas (1988) model. There, education was solely a function of the fraction of human capital the agent deviates from his work and allocates to studying. High real wages then implies a high opportunity cost of staying away from the labor market and thus, less education and less human capital formation.

Investment in schooling will also affect the transitional behavior of the economy as well as its steady-state dynamics. What happens is the following. In the Lucas model, the marginal product of the human capital devoted to studying is constant, being independent of real wages. Thus, throughout the transition, it is the return to holding assets that will have to do all the adjustment. The reason for this is intuitive: for every hour the agent spends in a public library, the amount of education he is going to get is always the same, being independent of what happens to real wages. Consequently, if the benefits of being better educated are higher than that of accumulating assets, the agent will work less and go to the library more. In general equilibrium, this causes interest rates to rise, in a process that will just terminate when the interest rate equals the constant net marginal product of studying. Notice that the education sector alone (the constant marginal product) determines the steady-state interest rate and thus the long-run growth rate of the economy.

This process changes considerably when education is also a function of investment in schooling. Now, the marginal product of the fraction of human capital devoted to studying is a positive function of the quality of the school the individual attends and hence, real wages. Therefore, throughout the transition, both the net return to holding assets as well as the net marginal product of studying will be adjusting. They will, in fact, converge to each other, being equalized whenever a steady-state is reached. Notice that the steady-state interest rate will be determined somewhere in the middle of the initial net return to holding assets and the initial net marginal product of studying, being a function of parameters describing both the education and consumption (assets) sectors of the economy.

Our analysis will be organized as follows. Section 1.2 describes the model and derives the first order conditions for the consumer and firm's problems. The main result of this section is that the return to accumulating human capital will be a function of real wages and, consequently, of the fraction of physical to human capital used in the production of the consumption good. This result ultimately implies that the dynamic behavior of the two-sector growth model can be characterized by a general tendency of returns to be equalized, with the individuals' decisions on how much to save, consume, and accumulate human capital, simply adjusting to this tendency. In more technical terms, the four dimensional non-linear differential system that characterizes the dynamics of the two-sector growth model, can be divided into a single non-linear differential equation (the tendency of returns to be equalized) and a three dimensional linear non-autonomous system (the adjustments in individuals's saving, consumption and human capital decisions). Section 1.3 takes a closer look at the transitional dynamics of the model. It is proved that, for linear homogeneous production functions, a steady-state will always exist and the economy will locally converge to it. Closed form expressions for the speed of convergence are then derived, and it is demonstrated that, whenever education requires investment in formal instruction, the economy will converge at a faster rate. Section 1.4 concentrates on long-run dynamics. At the steady-state equilibrium, consumer optimality implies that consumption as well as physical and human capital will all be growing at a common rate, which depends on parameters describing both the education and consumption sectors of the model. Moreover, this steady-state growth rate is a negative function of the relative price of formal instruction, so that economies for which schooling is inexpensive will tend to grow faster. Section 1.5 finally concludes the analysis.

Throughout the chapter we will be looking at three particular cases of the production function for human capital, and deriving results for each one of them. In the first case, education uniquely requires investment in formal instruction, with no need to deviate a fraction of human capital away from the labor market and towards studying. This case can be illustrated by an individual that goes to night school and allocates a portion of his leisure time to education. The second case is the Lucas model, and education just requires human capital being allocated to studying. The third and most important case describes what happens when education is both a function of investment in formal instruction as well as human capital devoted to studying.

1.2 The Model

1.2.1 Consumers

Consider a dynamic optimization problem in which a representative consumer facing an unbounded horizon has to maximize an intertemporal utility function Ω given by:

$$1)\ \Omega = L[0] \int_0^\infty U[c[t]].e^{-(\rho-n).t} dt$$

where $(\rho - n) > 0$ is the discount rate, $\rho > 0$ is the rate of time preference, n is the population growth rate, $c[t]$ is per-capita consumption at t, $L[t]$ is total population at t, and $U[c[t]]$ is the instantaneous utility function, which is increasing and concave in $c[t]$ and satisfies the Inada (1963) conditions.

At each period t the consumer receives wage income from the labor services he provides and interest income from the assets he owns. Total income is then used to finance expenditures in the consumption good, as well as investments in formal instruction. It will be assumed that assets and the consumption good are produced with the same technology, so that they govern the same price $P_c[t]$ which is normalized to 1.

The dynamic budget constraint for the consumer problem is given by the following equation:

2) $a'[t] = w[t].u[t].h[t] + (r[t]-n).a[t] - c[t] - P_b.b[t]$

The function $a[t]$ represents the consumer's total asset holdings, whereas $w[t]$ is the wage rate per-unit of human capital, $u[t]$ is the fraction of human capital allocated to working, $r[t]$ the real interest rate, P_b is the exogenously given unit price of formal instruction and $c[t]$ and $b[t]$ are, respectively, the consumer's total demand for the consumption good and the consumer's total demand for formal instruction.

Besides deciding on $c[t]$ and $b[t]$, at each period t the consumer has also to choose the fraction $(1-u[t])$ of his non-leisure-human-capital $h[t]$ to be allocated to studying rather than working[1]. By investing in formal instruction and allocating some human capital to studying, the consumer is able to increase future human capital and consequently future wage income. The process of producing human capital will be called "education" and it is assumed that the production function for human capital is given by:

3) $h'[t] = G\left[\left((1-u[t])h[t]\right), b[t]\right] - (\delta_h + n)h[t]$

where $(1-u[t])$ is the period t fraction of human capital allocated to studying and δ_h is the rate of depreciation of the human capital stock. The production function $G[.\,,.]$ satisfies the Inada (1963) conditions and is homogeneous of the first degree, with positive first order derivatives $G_1[.\,,.]$ and $G_2[.\,,.]$, and negative second order direct derivatives $G_{11}[.\,,.]$ and $G_{22}[.\,,.]$.

There are a few things to observe about equation 3). First of all, notice that in order to educate him/herself, the consumer needs to allocate a fraction $(1-u[t]).h[t])$ of human capital to studying and invest some real resources $b[t]$ in his/her formal instruction. Both of these "inputs" are substitutes in the education process, and a given level of education can be achieved either through a larger

---

[1] Since there is no labor-leisure choice in this model, $h[t]$ will be called "human capital", throughout the analysis. But it is important to bear in mind that $h[t]$ refers to the amount of human capital that remains to the consumer subsequently to his labor-leisure choice. For a two-sector growth model with endogenous labor see Benhabib and Perli (1994).

$b[t]$ and a lower $(1-u[t]).h[t])$ or vice-versa[2]. Secondly, the only way the consumer can increase the fraction $(1-u[t])$ of human capital allocated to studying is by decreasing by the same proportion the fraction $u[t]$ allocated to working. That is, the sort of education we will be looking at, is not derived from repeated working, or "on-the-job learning", but actually one of a more sophisticated type, in which the individual has to give up part of his working or leisure hours in order to go to school.

Two particular cases of equation 3) arise when the first order derivatives G_2 or G_1 are equal to zero. When $G_2 = 0$, the production function for human capital is linear on $(1-u[t]).h[t]$ and independent of the amount of real investment in formal instruction $b[t]$. That is, the consumer is able to educate him/herself just by dedicating some of his/her human capital to studying, with no need to go to school. This case was analyzed by Lucas (1988) and can be illustrated by a consumer dedicating a fraction of his/her working hours to go to the public library in order to educate him/herself. On the other hand, whenever $G_1 = 0$ the production function for human capital is linear on $b[t]$ and independent of $(1-u[t]).h[t])$. Thus, the consumer is able to educate him/herself just by investing in formal instruction, with no need to deviate part of his/her human capital away from the labor market and towards studying. This would be the case if, for instance, the consumer attended night school, to educate him/herself during his/her non-working hours.

1.2.1.1 The First-Order Conditions

The consumer problem P is to choose the time paths for consumption expenditure $c[t]$, real investment in formal instruction $b[t]$, and the fraction of human capital dedicated to working $u[t]$, so as to maximize the intertemporal utility function 1), given the wage rate $w[t]$, the interest rate $r[t]$, the price of formal instruction P_b, the initial stock of assets $a[0]$, the initial stock of human capital $h[0]$, and subject to the dynamic constraints 2) and 3), the non-negativity conditions $c[t] \geq 0$, $h[t] \geq 0$, the feasibility constraint $0 \leq u[t] \leq 1$ and the Non-Ponzi game condition:

---

[2] There is a set of iso-education curves in the space $[b[t],(1-u[t].h[t])]$. Consequently, in order to receive a given amount of education, the consumer can either go to an expensive school (which provides a larger $b[t]$) and dedicate less human capital to studying and more to working (low $(1-u[t]).h[t]$), or go to a inexpensive school (which provides a lower $b[t]$) and dedicate more human capital to studying and less to working (high $(1-u[t]).h[t]$).

$$4) \lim_{t \to \infty} a[t].e^{-\int_0^t (r[v]-n)dv} \geq 0$$

The first order conditions for the consumer problem are given by equations 5)-9):

$$5)\ c'[t]=c[t].\frac{1}{\theta[c[t]]}(r[t]-\rho), \quad \theta[c[t]]=-\frac{c[t]U''[c[t]]}{U'[c[t]]}$$

$$6)\ G_1[.,.] = \frac{w[t]}{P_b} G_2[.,.]$$

$$7)\ \frac{w'[t]}{w[t]} = \frac{\dfrac{\partial\ G_1[.,.]}{\partial\ t}}{G_1[.,.]} + r[t] - \left(G_1[.,.]+\delta_h\right)$$

$$8)\ \lim_{t \to \infty}\left[\frac{a'[t]}{a[t]}-(r[t]-n)\right]<0$$

$$9)\ \lim_{t \to \infty}\left[\frac{h'[t]}{h[t]}-(G_1[.,.]-\delta_h-n)\right]<0$$

Equation 5) is the traditional dynamic Euler condition, stating that whenever the return to holding assets is above (below) the rate of time preference, the consumer will be shifting consumption towards the future (present) at a rate which is a positive linear function of the elasticity of intertemporal substitution $1/\theta$ $[c[t]]$. Equation 6) is a static efficiency condition asserting that, at each t, the consumer will choose a combination of studying to real investment in formal instruction such that the marginal rate of transformation between these two inputs equal the relative price $w[t]/P_b$. Equation 7) deals with the dynamic allocation of human capital between working and studying. It states that, at each period t, the consumer will be adjusting the combination of studying to investing in formal instruction in such a way that the rate of increase of the net marginal benefit of studying equals the difference between period t returns to accumulating human capital and assets. Equations 8) and 9) are the usual transversality conditions. They state that if the boundary values of $a[t]$ and $h[t]$ are to be zero, it must be the case that the asymptotic rates at which assets and human capital are accumulated, are smaller than the respective asymptotic net returns.

1.2.1.2 Human Capital Accumulation

Equations 6) and 7) deserve special attention since they are non-existent in the traditional one-sector growth model[3]. They were derived from the first-order conditions with respect to the controls $u[t]$, $b[t]$ and the states $k[t]$, $h[t]$ and will be responsible for the most distinctive feature of the two-sector growth model, namely, steady-state growth.

The first thing to notice is that equation 6), together with the assumptions that the production function for education is linear homogeneous and satisfies the Inada (1963) conditions, imply that (i) whenever the marginal product of studying G_1 approaches zero, the fraction of human capital allocated to working goes to one; and that (ii) whenever the marginal product of investing in formal instruction G_2 approaches zero, real investment in schooling also goes to zero. The intuition for these results is clear. As $G_1 \to 0$, the production function for education converges to the "night school" production function, in which case education exclusively requires investment in formal instruction. Under these circumstances, there is no need for the consumer to deviate part of his/her non-leisure human capital away from working and towards studying so that $u[t] \to 1$. Conversely, as $G_2 \to 0$, the production function for education converges to the "public library" production function analyzed by Lucas (1988), in which case education exclusively requires that the individual allocates some fraction of his/her non-leisure human capital towards studying. Under these circumstances, there is no need for the consumer to invest real resources in going to school so that $b[t] \to 0$.

Secondly, notice that for the general case in which the first order derivatives G_1 and G_2 are non-zero, equation 6) and linear homogeneity of $G[.\,,.]$ implies that the combination of studying to real investment in formal instruction will be a negative function of $w[t]/P_b$ given by:

$$10) \quad \frac{(1-u[t]).h[t]}{b[t]} = E\left[\frac{w[t]}{P_b}\right], \quad E'\left[\frac{w[t]}{P_b}\right] < 0$$

---

3 In fact equations 6), 7) as well as 9) are absent in the traditional one-sector growth model (or Ramsey Model) as described in chapter 2 of Barro and Sala-i-Martin (1985). The transversality condition in 9), however, will turn out to be equal to the one in 8), so that the one-sector and two sector growth models will actually have the same transversality condition. The distinctive features of the two-sector model are then exclusively derived from equations 6) and 7).

That is, whenever the purchasing power of real wages in terms of schooling is high (low), the consumer will opt to go to a better (worse) school and allocate a higher fraction of his human capital towards working (studying).

The fact that the ratio $(1-u[t]).h[t]/b[t]$ is a negative function of $w[t]/P_b$ will be the distinguishing feature between the general "schooling" production function for education ($G_1 \neq 0$ and $G_2 \neq 0$), and the "night school" ($G_1 = 0$) and "public library" ($G_2 = 0$) production functions. The reason for this is that 10) and linear homogeneity of G imply that $G_1[.,.]$ and $G_2[.,.]$ are positive functions of $w[t]/P_b$, a result that is in sharp contrast to the constant marginal products that arise in the $G_1 = 0$ and $G_2 = 0$ cases.

The dynamic implications of equation 10) can be better visualized by a closer inspection of the intertemporal allocation condition in 7). For this, notice that 7) implies that, for the general "schooling" production function, whenever the return to accumulating assets is different from that of accumulating human capital, both wages as well as the marginal product of studying will be adjusting. Nonetheless, this will no longer be the case when one of the marginal products is equal to zero. In fact, for the "public library" production function analyzed by Lucas (1988), G_1 is going to be constant so that equation 7) can be rewritten as:

$$7') \frac{w'[t]}{w[t]} = r[t] - (G_1 + \delta_h)$$

That is, whenever the return to accumulating assets is different from that of accumulating human capital, the marginal product of studying remains constant and real wages do all the adjustment.

Similarly, for the "night school" production function, it is the marginal product of investing in schooling that is going to be constant. This fact, along with equation 2.6), allow us to rewrite equation 7) as:

$$7'') r[t] = \frac{w[t]}{P_b} G_2 - \delta_h$$

That is, at each period t, the consumer will choose a level of real investment in formal instruction such that the return to accumulating assets is exactly equal to that of accumulating human capital[4]. Notice that, since in this case the marginal benefit (G_2) as well as the marginal cost (P_b) of investing in formal instruction are constants, the consumer decision on $b'[t]/b[t]$ will be unaltered throughout the optimal path, so that what was formerly a dynamic allocation problem is reduced to a static one, with no need for $w[t]$ to adjust.

Finally, for the general case in which education requires both human capital being allocated to studying as well as real investment in formal instruction, linear homogeneity of $G[.\,,\,.]$ together with equation 10), allow us to rewrite 3) as:

$$3')\, h'[t] = B\left[E\left[\frac{w[t]}{P_b}\right]\right](1-u[t])h[t] - (\delta_h + n)h[t], \quad \frac{\partial\, B\left[E[w[t]/P_b]\right]}{\partial\, w[t]/P_b} > 0$$

where the function $B[E[w[t]/P_b]]$ is the average product of the human capital allocated to studying[5].

1.2.2 Firms

Firms produce the consumption good $Y[t]$ by hiring effective labor and renting physical capital from consumers. They face perfectly competitive good and factor markets and their technology is described by the following production function:

$$11)\, Y[t] = F[K[t], \ell[t]]$$

where $K[t]$ and $\ell[t]$ are, respectively, the stock of physical capital and the amount of effective labor hired by the firm. The production function $F[.\,,\,.]$

---

[4] For the $G_1 = 0$ production function, changes in real wages do not affect the fraction of human capital the consumer allocates to working, since he/she attends "night-school". In fact, as was already mentioned, $u[t] = 1$ throughout the optimal path.

[5] For the Lucas Model ($G_2 = 0$), the average product of the fraction of human capital allocated to studying will be constant and, in fact, equal to the marginal product G_1. The intuition for this result is the following. If the consumer educates him/herself by going to a public library and studying, then whenever real wage increases, he/she will spend less time in the library so as to be able to work more. However, for every hour he/she spends studying, the amount of education he/she is going to get is still the same. On the other hand, as it is clear from equation 3'), this will no longer be true when G_1 as well as G_2 are different than zero, in which case the consumer educates him/herself by going to school. Under these circumstances, the amount of per-hour education he/she receives by attending classes and studying at a top school, will be higher than what he/she would get if he/she could just afford an average school.

satisfies the Inada conditions and is homogeneous of the first degree, with positive first order derivatives $F_1[.\,,.]$ and $F_2[.\,,.]$, and negative second order direct derivatives $F_{11}[.\,,.]$ and $F_{22}[.\,,.]$.

Profit maximization guarantees that both inputs $K[t]$ and $\ell[t]$ will be employed up to the point at which their marginal products are equal to their marginal costs. The first-order conditions for the firm's problem are then given by:

12) $r[t] + \delta_k = F_1\big[d[t],\,1\big]$

13) $w[t] = F_2\big[d[t],\,1\big]$

where δ_k is the depreciation rate of the stock of physical capital and $d[t] = K[t]/\ell[t]$ is the ratio of physical capital to effective-labor used in the production of the consumption good.

1.2.3 General Equilibrium

In a closed economy, equilibrium will be reached when (i) the total number of assets purchased by consumers equals the aggregate capital stock rented by firms, (ii) the aggregate supply of human capital equals aggregated demand, and (iii) total expenditure by consumers is equal to the total production of the consumption good. These general equilibrium conditions are described in equations 14)-16) below:

14) $L[t].a[t] = K[t]$

15) $u[t].h[t].L[t] = \ell[t]$

16) $\big(a'[t] + c[t] + P_b[t].b[t] + n.a[t]\big)L[t] = Y[t] - \delta_k K[t]$

The per-capita stock of physical capital $K[t]/L[t]$ will be denoted by $k[t]$, so that equation 14) can be rewritten as:

14') $a[t] = k[t]$

Equations 15), 13), 10) and linear homogeneity of $G[.\,,.]$ imply that, for the general "schooling" production function, the marginal products $G_1[.\,,.]$ and $G_2[.\,,.]$ as well as the average product of studying $B[.]$ are going to be functions of $d[t]$, the fraction of physical to human capital employed in the production of the consumption good. That is:

$$17) \; G_1\left[(1-u[t])h[t],\, b[t]\right] = G_1\left[E\left[\frac{w[d[t]]}{P_b}\right],\, 1\right]$$

$$17') \; G_2\left[(1-u[t])h[t],\, b[t]\right] = G_2\left[E\left[\frac{w[d[t]]}{P_b}\right],\, 1\right]$$

$$17'') \; B\left[E\left[\frac{w[t]}{P_b}\right]\right] = B\left[E\left[\frac{w[d[t]]}{P_b}\right]\right]$$

If we now substitute 17) and 17'), as well as equations 12) and 13) into 7), we are able to derive the following nonlinear expression governing the time evolution of $d[t]$:

$$18) \; d'[t] = g[d[t]]$$

where, the exact form for 18) is given in Appendix 1.

Notice that equation 18) alone determines the steady-state fraction d^* of physical to human capital employed in the production of the consumption good[6]. This result is in sharp contrast to what happens in the traditional one-sector growth model, where d^* was determined by the dynamic Euler equation in 5)[7]. The reason for this is the following. For the case in which one single asset can be accumulated, the assumption of decreasing marginal products implies that the consumer' savings decision will just remain unchanged whenever the asset's return attains a lower bound. Consequently, in the one-sector growth model, a steady-state will be reached at the point where the real interest rate equals the rate of time preference. This, however, no longer needs to be true when more than one asset can be accumulated. Under these circumstances, the consumer's saving decision would also remain unchanged at the point at which assets returns are equalized and constant marginal products settles in. And in fact, this is exactly what happens in the two-sector growth model, where a steady-state is reached whenever the real interest rate equals the

---

[6] This result is immediate for the "night school" case, represented by equation A.1.3) in Appendix 1. However, for the "public library"($G_2 = 0$) and general "schooling" ($G_1 \neq 0$ and $G_2 \neq 0$) production functions represented by equations A.1.1) and A.1.2), it will latter be shown that $d[t]$ locally converges to d^*. See Proposition 1 and Corollary 1.1 below.

[7] The fact that d^* is completely determined by the intertemporal allocation equation in 18) is behind Santos and Ortigueira (1997) and Tenani (1997)'s finding that the speed of convergence for the two sector growth model does not depend on "utility" parameters. This result will be confirmed by Proposition 1 below. For a more complete analysis of this feature, see Chapter 2.

net marginal return to accumulating human capital, and there are constant marginal products to those factors that can be accumulated.

If one assumes a constant elasticity of substitution form for the instantaneous utility function[8] in 1), then equations 10), 12), 13) 14'), 17'') and the definition of $d[t]$ could be used to rewrite the dynamic system 2), 3') and 5) as the following linear but non-autonomous system of differential equations in $k[t]$, $h[t]$ and $c[t]$:

$$19) \begin{bmatrix} k'[t] \\ h'[t] \\ c'[t] \end{bmatrix} = \begin{bmatrix} A_{11}[d[t]] & -A_{12}[d[t]] & -1 \\ -A_{21}[d[t]] & A_{22}[d[t]] & 0 \\ 0 & 0 & A_{33}[d[t]] \end{bmatrix} \begin{bmatrix} k[t] \\ h[t] \\ c[t] \end{bmatrix}$$

where the expressions for the $A_{ij}[d[t]]$ terms are given in Appendix 2.

The nonlinear differential equation in 18) and the linear non-autonomous differential system in 22) describe the intertemporal market equilibrium of our economy. We now turn to the characterization of this equilibrium by looking at its transitional dynamics.

1.3 Transitional Dynamics

The transitional dynamics of the economy is completely characterized by the intertemporal allocation condition in 18), with $k[t]$, $h[t]$ and $c[t]$ then adjusting in the linear non-autonomous fashion described in 19). The account of this dynamics goes as follows. Whenever returns are not equalized, consumers will be shifting resources between accumulating real assets and human capital, so as to benefit the most from the highest return. In general equilibrium this alters factor prices, leading firms to adjust the fraction $d[t]$ of physical to human capital used in the production of the consumption good. Consumers then, facing modified returns, revise their portfolio decisions on how much assets and human capital to accumulate, which once again alter factor prices and lead firms to re-adjust $d[t]$. This process goes on "ad-infinitum" and, eventually, returns are equalized and the consumers as well as firms' decisions remain unchanged.

---

[8] Notice that d^*, and thus r^* and w^*, will be determined by equation 18) independently of the form of instantaneous utility function. However, if the steady-state elasticity of intertemporal substitution in consumption, $\theta^*[c[t]]$, is not constant, then the steady-state non-autonomous system in 19) will not be linear and the steady-state growth rates of $c[t]$, $k[t]$ and $h[t]$ will not be constant. For convenience of exposition, we then assume a CES utility function.

The important thing to observe about this account is that the transitional dynamics of the two sector growth model is also implicit in the behavior of $d[t]$, and not solely in the simultaneous behavior of $k[t]$, $h[t]$, $c[t]$ and $u[t]$[9]. That is, rather than looking at a very complicated economy where consumers accumulate both assets and human capital in addition to consume, work and study, one can also look at the global tendency for returns to be equalized, with the consumer's decision on $k[t]$, $h[t]$ and $c[t]$ merely adjusting to it.

The next step is to confirm that the returns to accumulating assets and human capital are eventually equalized. This is done in Proposition 1 below, with the particular cases of the "public library" and "night school" production functions dealt with in Corollaries 1.1 and 1.2.

Proposition 1: *The non-linear differential equation in 18) implies that the fraction $d[t]$ of physical to human capital used in the production of the consumption good, will locally[10] converge to a steady-state value d^* at speed λ.*

Proof: This result is immediate from taking a first-order Taylor expansion of $d'[t]$ around d^*, and confirming that the slope $-\lambda$ is negative. The steady-state value d^* is defined to be the point at which:

$$20) \quad F_1[d[t], 1] - \delta_k = G_1\left[E\left[\frac{w[d[t]]}{P_b}\right], 1\right] - \delta_h$$

so that returns are equalized and $d'[t] = 0$.

The speed of local convergence towards the steady-state[11] is given by the following expression:

---

9 Mulligan and Sala-i-Martin (1993) propose a different simplification for the dynamics of the two-sector model. Their idea is that, since at the steady-state the levels of $k[t]$, $h[t]$ and $c[t]$ will all be growing at a common rate, one would not lose much by concentrating on ratios rather than levels. The four dimensional dynamic system in $k[t]$, $h[t]$, $c[t]$ and $u[t]$ could then be reduced to a three dimensional system in $k[t]/h[t]$, $c[t]/k[t]$, and $u[t]$ which is considerably simpler. Tenani (1997) follows this approach to prove saddle path stability for a two-sector model of growth and education with Cobb-Douglas production functions.

10 To prove global convergence one would need some further assumptions on the third order derivatives of the production functions $G[.,.]$ and $F[.,.]$. For the Cobb-Douglas case, where $\eta_{F2,d}[d[t]]$ and $\eta_{G1,E}[w[t]/P_b]$ are constants and $\eta_{E,w/Pb}[w[t]/P_b] = -1$, it is possible to show that $d[t]$ will always converge to d^* for $d[0] < d^*$ and locally converge to d^* for $d[0] > d^*$.

11 If the production functions $G[.,.]$ and $F[.,.]$, take the Cobb-Douglas form, it can easily checked that 21) yields the same expression for the speed of convergence as the one derived by Tenani (1997).

$$21)\ \lambda = -\frac{d^*\left(F_1'[d^*,1] - \eta_{G_1,E}\left[\frac{w[d^*]}{P_b}\right]\eta_{E,w/P_b}\left[\frac{w[d^*]}{P_b}\right]\frac{G_1\left[E\left[\frac{w[d^*]}{P_b}\right],1\right]}{d^*}\right)}{\eta_{F_2,d}[d^*]\left(1 - \eta_{G_1,E}\left[\frac{w[d^*]}{P_b}\right]\eta_{E,w/P_b}\left[\frac{w[d^*]}{P_b}\right]\right)}$$

And notice that, λ does neither depend on the discount rate nor on the elasticity of intertemporal substitution in consumption, which is in clear contrast to what happens in the one-sector growth model.

Corollary 1.1: *For the "public library" ($G_2 = 0$) production function analyzed by Lucas (1988), the non-linear differential equation in 18) implies that the fraction d[t] of physical to human capital used in the production of the consumption good, will locally converge to a steady-state value d^* at speed λ_1.*

Proof: This result is immediate from taking a first-order Taylor expansion of $d'[t]$ around d^* and confirming that the slope $-\lambda_1$ is negative. The steady-state value d^* is defined to be the point at which:

$$20')\ F_1[d[t],1] - \delta_k = G_1 - \delta_h$$

so that returns are equalized and $d'[t] = 0$.

The speed of local convergence[12] towards the steady-state is given by the following expression:

$$21')\ \lambda_1 = -\frac{d^* F_1'[d^*,1]}{\eta_{F_2,d}[d^*]}$$

There are a few things to observe about the results in Proposition 1 and Corollary 1.1. First of all, notice that, for the general case in which education

---

12 If the production function F[.,.], takes the Cobb-Douglas form, it can be easily checked that 21') yields the same expression for the speed of convergence as the one derived in Ortigueira and Santos (1997).

requires both studying as well as investment in formal instruction, the transitional dynamics of the economy will be characterized by an interest rate that converges to the net marginal benefit of accumulating human capital and vice-versa. However, this will no longer be true for the "public library" production function, where studying is the sole input to the education process. Under these circumstances, the marginal benefit of accumulating human capital is constant so that the interest rate will have to do all the adjustment[13].

The second thing to notice is that if we normalize the steady-state level of $d[t]$ to be the same for the general and public library production functions, then the ratio of λ to λ_1 will be given by:

$$22) \frac{\lambda}{\lambda_1} = \frac{\left(F_1'[.,.] - \eta_{G_1,E}[.] \eta_{E,w/P_b}[.] \frac{G_1[.,.]}{d^*}\right)}{F_1'[.,.]} \frac{1}{\left(1 - \eta_{G_1,E}[.] \, \eta_{E,w/P_b}[.]\right)} > 1$$

Equation 22) implies that the speed of conditional convergence is higher whenever education requires both studying as well as investment in formal instruction. And the intuition for this result is clear: if both interest rates as well as the return to accumulating human capital adjust to the consumer's portfolio decisions, $d[t]$ will converge towards d^* at a higher rate than if interest rates alone had to do the entire adjustment.

Corollary 1.2 below deals with the transitional dynamics for the "night school" case, in which education exclusively requires investment in formal instruction, with no need for the consumer to deviate human capital away from the labor market and towards studying.

Corollary 1.2: *For the "night school" production function ($G_1 = 0$), the nonlinear differential equation 18) implies that the fraction $d[t]$ of physical to human capital used in the production of the consumption good will always be at its steady-state value d^*.*

Proof: This result is immediate from equation A.1.3) in Appendix 1.

---

13 These distinct transitional dynamics will have important long-run implications. In fact, for the "general schooling" production function, the steady-state growth rate will be a function of parameters describing both the education and consumption good sectors, whereas for the "public library" case, the education sector alone will determine long-run growth. See Propositions 4 and 5.

Proposition 1 as well as Corollaries 1.2 and 1.3, imply that in order to get out-of-steady-state dynamics we need $G_1 \neq 0$. The reason for this is the following. Whenever $G_1 \neq 0$ and education requires that human capital be allocated to studying, the consumer's decision on how much education to get will affect the relative supply of human capital available to firms and thus, factor returns $r[t]$ and $w[t]$. A change in factor returns will then alter the firms' decision on $d[t]$, in a process that will go on until a steady-state is eventually reached. On the other hand, whenever $G_1 = 0$, this is no longer true. In this case, education is solely a function of investment in formal instruction and the consumer allocates all his human capital to working. There is no effect whatsoever from the consumer's decision on how much education to get, on the relative amount of human capital supplied to firms, and thus real wages and interest rates. Since factor returns remain constant, so will the firms' decision on $d[t]$ and the $G_1 = 0$ economy is always on its steady-state equilibrium.

1.4 Steady-state Equilibrium

Once the global tendency for returns to be equalized has been confirmed, let's turn to the characterization of the steady-state dynamics and how the consumer's decisions on $a[t]$, $h[t]$, $c[t]$ and $u[t]$ adjust to this tendency. Throughout the section, the steady-state values will be denoted by a star (" * ") superscript.

Proposition 2: *Whenever $G_1 \neq 0$ and education requires non-leisure human capital being allocated to studying, $u[t]$ will ultimately converge to a constant value u^*, whereas the rates of growth of $k[t]$, $h[t]$ and $c[t]$ will converge to a common and constant rate $\gamma[d^*]$.*

Proof: For $d[t] = d^*$, the solutions to the linear system in 19) must be of the following form:

23) $k^*[t] = \Psi_0 . e^{\gamma[d^*].t} + \Psi_1 . e^{\gamma_1[d^*].t} + \Psi_2 . e^{\gamma_2[d^*].t}$

24) $h^*[t] = \Psi_0 . x_2\left[d^*\right] . e^{\gamma[d^*].t} + \Psi_1 . v_2\left[d^*\right] . e^{\gamma_1[d^*].t} + \Psi_2 . m_2 . e^{\gamma[d^*].t}$

25) $c^*[t] = \Psi_0 . x_3\left[d^*\right] . e^{\gamma[d^*].t}$

where Ψ_1, Ψ_2 and Ψ_3 are arbitrary constants; $\gamma[d^*]$, $\gamma_1[d^*]$, $\gamma_2[d^*]$ are the eigenvalues of the matrix in 19); and $x_i[d^*]$, $v_i[d^*]$, $m_i[d^*]$ are, respectively, the ith

Human Capital and Growth 19

element of the eigenvectors correspondent to the $\gamma[d^*]$, $\gamma_1[d^*]$, $\gamma_2[d^*]$ eigenvalues[14]; all being evaluated at $d[t] = d^*$.

Not all the solutions specified in 23)-25), however, will satisfy the optimality conditions for the consumer problem *P*. To rule out these solutions note that, from Appendix 2, the eigenvalues $\gamma_1[d^*]$ and $\gamma_2[d^*]$ have both positive real parts. Therefore, if the arbitrary constants Ψ_2 and Ψ_3 are different than zero, the consumer will end up accumulating assets at a different rate than the rate at which consumption expenditure is increased. Two possibilities may arise: i) if $a^{*'}[t]/a^*[t] < c^{*'}[t]/c^*[t]$, then $c^*[t]/a^*[t] \to \infty$ and, from 2) and 14'), $k^{*'}[t]/k^*[t] \to -\infty$. Thus, after a while, $K[t] = 0$ and none of the consumption good will be produced. At this point, the consumer has to abruptly reduce consumption expenditures, and the dynamic Euler equation in 5) is violated;

ii) if $a^{*'}[t]/a^*[t] > c^{*'}[t]/c^*[t]$, then $c^*[t]/a^*[t] \to 0$ and, from 2), 10), 12) and 13), $a^{*'}[t]/a^*[t] = w[d^*]/d^* + (r[d^*] - n) + P_b.b^*[t]/a^*[t]$[15]. Since both $b^*[t]$ and $a^*[t]$[16] are non-negative, such a rate of asset accumulation is above $(r[d^*] - n)$, and the transversality condition in 8) is violated.

$$23') \; k^*[t] = \Psi_0 . e^{\gamma[d^*]t}$$

$$24') \; h^*[t] = \Psi_0 \left\{ \frac{A_{21}[d^*]}{\left(A_{22}[d^*] - \gamma^*[d^*]\right)} \right\} . e^{\gamma[d^*]t}$$

$$25') \; c^*[t] = \Psi_0 \left\{ \left(A_{11}[d^*] - \gamma[d^*]\right) - \frac{A_{12}[d^*]A_{21}[d^*]}{\left(A_{22}[d^*] - \gamma[d^*]\right)} \right\} . e^{\gamma[d^*]t}$$

Since possibilities i) and ii) violate either the dynamic Euler equation or the transversality condition, it must be the case that $a^{*'}[t]/a^*[t] = c^{*'}[t]/c^*[t]$ and,

---

14 The closed form expressions for $\gamma[d^*]$, $\gamma_1[d^*]$, $\gamma_2[d^*]$, $x_i[d^*]$, $v_i[d^*]$, $m_i[d^*]$ are derived in Appendix 2. Notice that, when writing equation 25, it was already taken into account that $v_3[d^*] = m_3[d^*] = 0$.
15 For the "public library" production function, the consumer will not invest any resources in formal instruction, so that $b[t] = 0$ for any t. Real assets will then end up being accumulated at the rate $a^{*'}[t]/a^*[t] = w[d^*]/d^* + (r[d^*] - n)$, which also violates the transversality condition.
16 The Non-Ponzi Game condition in 4) as well as the market-equilibrium condition 14) will imply that $a^*[t] \geq 0$. For further discussion, see Chapter 2 of Barro and Sala-i-Martin (1995).

from 23) and 24), $\Psi_1 = \Psi_2 = 0$[17]. Substituting $\Psi_1 = \Psi_2 = 0$ into 23), 24) and 25), one can derive the exact form of those solutions to 19) which also satisfy consumer's optimality:

$$23') \ k^*[t] = \Psi_0 \cdot e^{\gamma[d^*]t}$$

$$24') \ h^*[t] = \Psi_0 \left\{ \frac{A_{21}[d^*]}{(A_{22}[d^*] - \gamma^*[d^*])} \right\} \cdot e^{\gamma[d^*]t}$$

$$25') \ c^*[t] = \Psi_0 \left\{ (A_{11}[d^*] - \gamma[d^*]) - \frac{A_{12}[d^*]A_{21}[d^*]}{(A_{22}[d^*] - \gamma[d^*])} \right\} \cdot e^{\gamma[d^*]t}$$

where the expressions for $x_i[d^*]$ were substituted from Appendix 2 and the common rate of growth of $k[t]$, $h[t]$ and $c[t]$ is given by:

$$26) \ \gamma[d^*] = \frac{1}{\theta} \left(F_1[d^*, 1] - \delta_k - \rho \right)$$

To prove that $u[t]$ converges to a constant, just notice that, if $d[t] = d^*$ and $k^{*'}[t]/k^*[t] = h^{*'}[t]/h^*[t]$, then, by the definition of $d[t]$, it must be the case that $u[t] = u^*$[18].

Proposition 2 confirms that, for the "general" ($G_1 \neq 0$ and $G_2 \neq 0$) and "public library" ($G_2 = 0$) production functions, the global tendency for returns to be equalized will ultimately lead the economy to a resting state at which $u[t]$ as well as the ratios $h[t]/k[t]$ and $c[t]/k[t]$ remain constant[19]. The common rate of growth of $k^*[t]$ and $c^*[t]$, however, will no longer be zero, as it was the case in

---

17 Notice that, up to this point, the argument does not depend on the elasticity of intertemporal substitution in consumption being constant. That is, it will always be true that $d[t] \to d^*$, and $k'[t]/k[t] = h'[t]/h[t] = c'[t]/c[t]$. In fact, the constant elasticity of substitution assumption will solely imply that the common growth rate, $\gamma[t] = (F_1[d^*, 1] - \delta_k - \rho)/\theta$, is also constant.
18 Equation 10), together with the fact that d^* as well as u^* are constants and that $h^{*'}[t]/h^*[t]$ grow at the rate $\gamma[d^*] = (F_1[d^*, 1] - \delta_k - \rho)/\theta$ imply that, for the "general schooling" ($G_1 \neq 0$, $G_2 \neq 0$) production function, real investment in formal instruction $b[t]$ will also grow at the common rate $\gamma[d^*]$.
19 Notice that, from 23'), 24') and 25'), one can derive closed form expressions for the steady-state ratios $h^*[t]/k^*[t]$ and $c^*[t]/k^*[t]$ as functions of d^*.

the one-sector growth model, but actually positive[20]. And the reason for this has to do with the fact that, in the two-sector model, both inputs to the production of the consumption good can be accumulated. Therefore decreasing marginal products never settles in, and the interest rate will never reach the lower bound given by the rate of time preference.

The steady-state features of the $G_1 \neq 0$ production functions carry over to the $G_1 = 0$ case, with the distinction that the "night school" economy is always on its steady-state equilibrium. This is shown in Proposition 3 below.

Proposition 3: *Whenever education uniquely requires investment in formal instruction, $u[t]$ will always be at its steady-state constant value u^*, and $k[t]$, $h[t]$ and $c[t]$ will always grow at the constant rate $\gamma[d^*]$.*

Proof: By an argument similar to the one in Proposition 2, it can be shown that $k[t]$ and $(c[t] + P_b.b[t])$ will be growing at the same rate. Moreover, from equation 3) we also have that $b'[t]/b[t] = h'[t]/h[t]$. These two facts, combined with Corollary 1.2, allow us to conclude that $b'[t]/b[t] = k'[t]/k[t] = h'[t]/h[t] = c'[t]/c[t] = \gamma[d^*]$ and $u[t] = u^*$. Finally, from the dynamic Euler equation and the assumption of a constant marginal rate of intertemporal substitution, one gets that $\gamma[d^*]$ is a constant equal to $(F_1[d^*, 1]-\delta_k - \rho)/\theta$.

Propositions 2 and 3 indicate that the "general schooling" ($G_1 \neq 0$, $G_2 \neq 0$), "public library" ($G_2 = 0$) and "night school" ($G_1 = 0$) production functions will all deliver steady-state growth. However, the way in which the steady-state interest rate, and consequently $\gamma[d^*]$, is determined in each of these cases, will turn out to be dependent on whether education requires or not investment in formal instruction. This feature is analyzed in Propositions 4 and 5 below.

Proposition 4: *Whenever $G_2 = 0$ and education exclusively requires human capital being allocated to studying, the steady-state interest rate will be determined by the education sector alone, being independent of parameters describing the consumption sector of the economy.*

---

20 Negative growth rates can be ruled out since, by a similar argument to the one used in Proposition 2, the dynamic Euler equation in 5) will be violated whenever $K[t] = 0$. A zero growth rate, on the other hand, can only occur in the very particular case in which parameter values are such that $F_1[d^*, 1] - \delta_k = \rho$.

Proof: From 20') one gets that the steady-state interest rate will equal the exogenously given marginal return to accumulating human capital, $G_1 - \delta_h$.

Proposition 5: *Whenever $G_2 \neq 0$ and education requires investment in formal instruction, the steady-state interest rate will depend on parameters describing both the consumption and education sectors of the economy.*

Proof: From 20') and A.3.1) one gets that, for the "general schooling" and "night school" production functions, the steady-state fraction of physical to human capital used in the production of the consumption good will be a function of parameters describing both the education and consumption good sectors of the economy. Equation 12) then implies that the steady-state interest rate will also be a function of these parameters.

The differences that arise in the determination of the steady-state interest rate for the $G_2 = 0$ and $G_2 \neq 0$ economies, have to do with the distinct roles played by real wages in the education process. What happens is the following. Whenever education requires investment in formal instruction, changes in real wages will affect the quality of the school the consumer can afford and consequently, the marginal return to accumulating human capital. Therefore, the education as well as the consumption good (wages) sectors, will both interact in determining the steady-state interest rate, and thus steady-state growth. This, however, will no longer be true for the $G_2 = 0$ economy, where the consumer educates himself by going to a public library. In this case, changes in real wages will not affect the marginal return to accumulating human capital, but only the fraction of human capital allocated to studying. In this sense, the education sector alone (the constant marginal product) determines the steady-state interest rate and thus, steady-state growth.

To conclude the analysis, Proposition 6 reveals how the steady-state growth rate is affected by changes in the price of schooling.

Proposition 6: *Whenever $G_2 \neq 0$, the steady-state growth rate is a negative function of the price of formal instruction.*

Proof: By totally differentiating 20') and A.3.1) it is possible to show that, for the "general schooling" and "night school" economies, $\Delta d^*/\Delta P_b > 0$. Equations 12) and 26) then implies that $\Delta \gamma [d^*]/\Delta P_b < 0$.

The intuition for the result that long-term growth is negatively related to the price of schooling is the following. Whenever P_b is high, the purchasing power of real wages in terms of formal instruction will be small, so that the consumer can only afford to attend low-quality schools. This implies that the marginal return to accumulating human capital will be smaller, which decreases the steady-state interest rate and causes both physical as well as human capital to be accumulated at a lower rate. Therefore, those economies for which the price of formal instruction is high, will tend to accumulate less physical and human capital and, consequently, grow at lower rates.

1.5 Conclusion

This chapter presented a general formulation of the two-sector growth model in which education requires investment in formal instruction as well as human capital being allocated to studying. Under these circumstances, the marginal return to accumulating human capital is a function of the quality of the school attended by individuals and thus, the purchasing power of real wages in terms of schooling.

As the economy evolves towards its steady-state, the return to accumulating human capital converges to that of holding assets and vice-versa. Whenever these returns are equalized a steady-state is reached. The economy then grows at a rate that is a function of parameters describing both the consumption and education sectors of the model, and depends negatively on the relative price of schooling.

Chapter 2

On the Speedy of Convergence of Economic Growth Models

Contrary to what happens in the traditional Solow model, the speed of convergence at which the two-sector economy converges to its steady-state equilibrium is solely a function of technological parameters, being independent of consumer preferences. The reason for this is that, in the two sector framework – during the transitional dynamics – the central planner problem is to decide on which factor to accumulate most, which is in sharp contrast to the traditional consumption-accumulation decision of the Solow model.

2.1 Introduction

Contrary to what happens in the traditional Solow-Ramsey one-sector growth model, the speed at which the two-sector economy locally converges towards its steady-state equilibrium is solely a function of the production technology, being independent of preference parameters such as the discount rate and the rate of intertemporal substitution in consumption. The reason for this is that, by allowing both factors of production to be accumulated, the two-sector framework adds another dimension to the "consumption-accumulation" decision of the Solow-Ramsey model. Now, apart from having to decide on how much output to consume and accumulate, the central planner has also to choose which factor of production to accumulate most. The transitional dynamics of the system is completely characterized by this technological decision, with the central planner shifting resources towards the factor that yields the highest return.

Once returns are equalized, the two-sector economy reaches a steady state. From this point on, the planner's problem is reduced to the "consumption-accumulation" decision of the Solow-Ramsey economy so that, in the two-sector framework, it is the steady-state dynamics, rather than the transition, which is affected by preference parameters.

The chapter is organized as follows. Section 2.2 examines the Solow-Ramsey model and explains how the planner's "consumption-accumulation" decision completely defines the transitional dynamics of the system. The main intuition is that, with only one factor being accumulated, the convergence towards the steady-state is characterized by a continuous measurement of the return to factor accumulation against the cost of postponing consumption. That is, the speed of convergence will be a function of preference as well as technological parameters. Section 2.3 introduces the two-sector framework and allows for both factors of production to be accumulated. Under these circumstances, the transition will be characterized by the return to accumulating one factor being measured against the return to accumulating the other factor, rather than the cost of postponing consumption. This implies that the speed of convergence is solely a function of the production technology, being independent of preference parameters. Section 2.3 concludes the analysis.

All the results referred in the text are proved in Appendix 3 and 4, for the cases of linear homogeneous production technologies and a strictly concave instantaneous utility function. The assumption of a constant elasticity of intertemporal substitution in consumption, in particular, is only required in the two-sector framework, in order to generate steady-state growth. It is unnecessary for the analysis of the transitional dynamics of both the Solow-Ramsey as well as the two-sector growth models.

2.2 The Speed of Convergence in the Neoclassical Growth Model

Consider the traditional infinite-horizon Solow-Ramsey one-sector growth model, in which a central planner maximizes an intertemporal utility function Ω subject to a dynamic budget constraint and two non-negativity conditions:

1) $Max \ \Omega = \int_0^\infty U[c[t]] \ e^{-\rho t} dt$

2) $k'[t] = F[k[t], h] - c[t]$

3) $c[t] \geq 0, \ k[t] \geq 0$

The instantaneous utility function $U[.]$ is increasing and concave in $c[t]$ whereas the production function for total output, $F[.,.]$, is homogeneous of the first degree in the stocks of physical capital $k[t]$ and human capital h, with positive first-order derivatives $F_1[.,.]$ and $F_2[.,.]$, and negative second-order direct derivatives $F_{11}[.,.]$ and $F_{22}[.,.]$. The positive rate of time preference is denoted by ρ, and both the instantaneous utility function $U[.]$ as well as the production function $F[.,.]$ satisfy the Inada (1963) conditions. The control and state variables are, respectively, consumption $c[t]$ and physical capital $k[t]$, with the stock of human capital h assumed to be constant. The consumption good as well as physical capital are produced with the same technology $F[.,.]$ and have the same price $p[.]$, which is normalized to one.

The first-order conditions for the Solow-Ramsey problem are given by:

4) $c'[t] = c[t] \dfrac{1}{\theta[c[t]]} (F_1[.,.] - \rho),$

where $\theta[c[t]] = -\dfrac{c[t] U''[c[t]]}{U'[c[t]]} > 0$

5) $\lim_{t \to \infty} \left(\dfrac{k'[t]}{k[t]} - F_1[.,.] \right) < 0$

Equation 4) is the dynamic Euler condition stating that whenever the return to accumulating physical capital is above (below) the rate of time preference ρ, consumption $c[t]$ will be shifted towards the future (present) at a rate which is a positive linear function of the elasticity of intertemporal substitution $1/\theta\,[c[t]]$. Equation 5) is the usual transversality condition. It asserts that if the boundary value of physical capital is to be zero, it must be the case that the asymptotic rate at which $k[t]$ is accumulated is smaller than its asymptotic return.

As shown in Appendix 3, the assumptions that the production function $F[.,.]$ is linear homogeneous, that the second derivative $F_{11}[.,.]$ is negative and that the stock of human capital h is constant, will ultimately imply that the two-dimension non-linear differential system in equations 2) and 4) locally converges to a resting state where $c'[t] = k'[t] = 0$ and the levels of consumption and physical capital remain unaltered at c^* and k^*. The intuition for this result is the following. As physical capital is accumulated, the ratio $k[t]/h$ of inputs used in the production of total output $F[.,.]$ increases, thus reducing the marginal product of physical capital $F_1[.,.]$ until a boundary, given by the rate of time preference ρ, is reached. From this point on, the totality of output $F[.,.]$ is consumed and no physical capital is accumulated. The central planner decisions remain unaltered and a steady state is reached.

Appendix 3 also shows that the steady-state equilibrium of the Solow-Ramsey economy is unique as well as locally saddle path stable. Moreover, the speed at which $c[t]$ and $k[t]$ locally converge to their steady-state values, c^* and k^*, is given by[1]:

$$6)\ \beta = -\frac{1}{2}F_1\left[k^*,h\right]\left\{1-\sqrt{1+4\frac{1}{\theta\left[c^*\right]}\frac{\eta_{F_1,k}\left[k^*,h\right]}{\omega_k\left[k^*,h\right]}}\right\} > 0$$

Where the elasticity of the marginal product of physical capital with respect to $k[t]$ is denoted by $\eta_{F_1,k}[.,.]$ and the physical capital share of total output is denoted by $\omega_k[.,.]$.

---

1 As it is clear from Appendix 1, there is no need to assume a constant coefficient for the elasticity of intertemporal substitution in consumption, $\theta\,[c[t]] = \theta$, in order to derive the steady-state and dynamic properties of the Solow-Ramsey Model. See Barro and Sala-i-Martin (1995) for further discussions on the Solow-Ramsey Model and the derivation of the speed of convergence for Cobb-Douglas technology and CES instantaneous utility function.

Notice that, from equation 6), the speed of convergence β is a function of preference as well as technology parameters. The reason for this is that, during the transition, the central planner continuously measures the return to accumulating physical capital against the cost of postponing consumption, so as to adjust his optimal consumption and accumulation decisions. In this sense, technological parameters such as $F_1[.,.]$, $\eta_{F1,k}[.,.]$ and $\omega_k[.,.]$, which represent the benefit of accumulating $k[t]$, will interact with preference or "consumption" parameters such as $\theta[.]$ and ρ, so as to determine the speed at which the Solow-Ramsey economy converges towards its steady-state equilibrium.

Equation 6) also specifies the exact form in which the various parameters of the model affect the speed of convergence β. The results are as follows. (i) A large marginal product $F_1[.,.]$ indicates a large return to accumulating physical capital, so that present consumption is swapped for $k[t]$ at a higher rate. Because of decreasing marginal products, this ultimately leads to a faster convergence of $F_1[.,.]$ towards its steady-state value ρ. (ii) A high elasticity $\eta_{F1,k}[.,.]$ means that the marginal product of physical capital is sensitive to changes in $k[t]$. Consequently, any given increase in the stock of physical capital will cause $F_1[.,.]$ to converge towards ρ at a faster rate β. (iii) A large rate of intertemporal substitution $\theta[.]$ implies that, for any given out-of-steady-state position $F_1[.,.] \neq \rho$, the rate of growth of consumption will be smaller, causing $c[t]$ to converge towards c^* at a lower speed. (iv) Finally, a large physical capital share $\omega_k[.,.]$ indicates that total output $F[.,.]$ is sensitive to changes in $k[t]$. Consequently, for any given increase in the stock of physical capital, output will augment slightly, causing the next period $k'[t]$ to be small and $k[t]$ to converge towards k^* at a lower rate β.

Section 2.3 below relaxes the assumption that h is constant and allows for both physical as well as human capital to be accumulated. Under these circumstances the speed of convergence is solely a function of technology parameters, being independent of ρ and $\theta[.]$. Preference parameters, however, will have an important role in determining the steady-state dynamics of the model, a feature that is non-existent in the zero-steady-state-growth Solow-Ramsey economy.

2.3 The Speed of Convergence in the Two-Sector Growth Model

Consider the following infinite-horizon dynamic-optimization problem in which a central planner maximizes an intertemporal utility function Ω subject to a dynamic budget constraint, a human capital accumulation condition, as well as three non-negativity constraints and two consistency conditions:

$$7) \ Max \ \Omega = \int_0^\infty U[c[t]] e^{-\rho t} dt$$

$$8) \ k'[t] = F[\eta[t]k[t], u[t]h[t]] - c[t]$$

$$9) \ h'[t] = G\left[(1-\eta[t])k[t], (1-u[t])h[t]\right]$$

$$10) \ c[t] \geq 0, \ k[t] \geq 0, \ h[t] \geq 0$$

$$11) \ 0 \leq u[t] \leq 1, \ 0 \leq \eta[t] \leq 1$$

The production functions $F[.,.]$ and $G[.,.]$ both satisfy the Inada (1963) conditions and are homogeneous of the first degree with positive first-order derivatives $F_1[.,.]$, $F_2[.,.]$, $G_1[.,.]$ and $G_2[.,.]$ and negative second-order direct derivatives $F_{11}[.,.]$, $F_{22}[.,.]$, $G_{11}[.,.]$ and $G_{22}[.,.]$. The control variables are consumption $c[t]$, and the fractions $\eta[t]$ and $u[t]$ of physical and human capital allocated in the production of total output $F[.,.]$, whereas the state variables are the stocks of physical and human capital $k[t]$ and $h[t]$. All other assumptions remain as specified in Section 2.

The two-sector growth model as described by 7)-11) introduces a couple of modifications to the Solow-Ramsey framework. (i) The first one has to do with the fact that the functions $F[.,.]$ and $G[.,.]$ both contain $k[t]$ and $h[t]$ as arguments[2], so that the production of total output and human capital are competing activities. In this sense, the central planner's static input allocation decisions will be such that the ratio $(1-\eta[t])k[t]/((1-u[t])h[t])$, of physical to human capital used in the production of $h[t]$, is a function of the ratio $\eta[t]k[t]/(u[t]h[t])$, of physical to human capital used in the production of total output[3]. (ii) The second modification has to do with the fact that, in the two-sector framework, both inputs can be accumulated[4]. This will lead the central planner to shift resources between accumulating $k[t]$ and $h[t]$ for as long as the

---

[2] In the Solow-Ramsey model, the stock of human capital is given, so that the production function $G[.,.]$ is a constant given by $G[.,.] = h$.

[3] This is a consequence of the fact that the optimal static allocation of inputs is such that the marginal rates of transformation of $k[t]$ and $h[t[$ are equalized. See Proposition 3 in Appendix 2.

[4] The assumptions that both factors of production can be accumulated, that the production functions are linear homogeneous and that the instantaneous utility function is of the constant elasticity of intertemporal substitution form, will ultimately imply steady-state growth. This is a well-known result and will not be commented any further. See Barro and Sala-i-Martin (1995).

return $F_1[.,.]$, of allocating physical capital to the production of total output, differs from the return $G_2[.,.]$, of allocating human capital to the production of human capital. That is, it is no longer the case that the transitional dynamics towards the steady-state is characterized by the return to accumulating $k[t]$ being measured against the cost of postponing consumption, as it was the case in the Solow-Ramsey economy. Instead, in the two-sector framework, the transition is characterized by the return to accumulating physical capital being measured against that of accumulating human capital, leaving preference parameters completely out of the determination of the speed of convergence[5].

The above modifications result in three additional first-order conditions that, in conjunction with equations 4) and 5), describe the optimal solution to the planner's problem in 7)-11). These conditions are as follows:

$$12)\ \frac{G_1\left[\frac{(1-\eta[t])k[t]}{(1-u[t])h[t]},1\right]}{G_2\left[\frac{(1-\eta[t])k[t]}{(1-u[t])h[t]},1\right]} = \frac{F_1\left[\frac{\eta[t]k[t]}{u[t]h[t]},1\right]}{F_2\left[\frac{\eta[t]k[t]}{u[t]h[t]},1\right]}$$

$$13)\ G_2[.,.] - F_1[.,.] = \frac{\partial G_2[.,.]/\partial t}{G_2[.,.]} - \frac{\partial F_2[.,.]/\partial t}{F_2[.,.]}$$

$$14)\ \lim_{t \to \infty}\left(\frac{h'[t]}{h[t]} - G_2[.,.]\right) < 0$$

Equation 12) is a static efficiency condition asserting that, at each t, the fractions $\eta[t]$ and $u[t]$ will be chosen in such a way that the marginal rates of transformation of $k[t]$ into $h[t]$ are equalized among the alternative uses of producing total output and human capital. Notice that, in writing equation 12), it was already taken into account that $F[.,.]$ and $G[.,.]$ are homogeneous functions. Equation 13) deals with the intertemporal allocation of $k[t]$ and $h[t]$. It asserts that whenever the marginal benefit of accumulating $h[t]$ is above (below) that of accumulating $k[t]$, it must be the case that the marginal opportunity cost of accumulating $h[t]$ is increasing by less (more) than the marginal benefit. Notice that, as shown in Proposition A.4.2 in Appendix 4, the

---

5   Ortigueira and Santos (1997) rely on Mulligan and Sala-i-Martin (1993) to derive another interpretation for the fact that, in the two-sector growth model with Cobb-Douglas Production Functions, the speed of convergence is independent of preference parameters. We refer to their original article for further clarifications on their approach.

assumption that $F[.,.]$ and $G[.,.]$ are linear homogeneous functions will ultimately imply that equation 13) is a nonlinear differential equation in the input ratio $(\eta[t]k[t])/(u[t]h[t])$. Equation 14) is the usual transversality condition stating that, if the boundary value of $h[t]$ is to be zero, the asymptotic rates at which $h[t]$ is accumulated must be smaller than its asymptotic return.

In Appendix 4 it is shown that under certain conditions on the instantaneous utility function $U[.]$ and on the elasticities of the marginal products $F_1[.,.]$ and $G_2[.,.]$, the two-sector economy will eventually reach a resting state where the returns to accumulating $k[t]$ and $h[t]$ are equalized, the fractions $\eta[t]$ and $u[t]$ remain constant, and consumption, as well as physical and human capital all grow at a common rate $\gamma[d^*]$. Moreover, the speed at which the two-sector economy locally converges to this steady-state equilibrium[6] is given by:

$$15)\ \beta\left[d^*\right] = -\left(\frac{G_2\left[E\left[d^*\right],1\right]F_2\left[d^*,1\right]}{F_2\left[d^*,1\right]G_{21}\left[E\left[d^*\right],1\right] - G_2\left[E\left[d^*\right],1\right]F_{21}\left[d^*,1\right]}\right)\left(G_{21}\left[E\left[d^*\right],1\right] - F_{11}\left[d^*,1\right]\right)$$

where d^* denotes the steady-state physical to human capital ratio $(\eta[t]k[t])/(u[t]h[t])$ used in the production of total output $F[.,.]$ and the function $E[d[t]]$ is defined in Proposition 3, Appendix 4.

Notice from equation 15) that the speed of convergence $\beta[d^*]$ is solely a function of the production technology $F[.,.]$ and $G[.,.]$, being independent of preference parameters such as θ and ρ. This result is a direct consequence of the fact that, in the two-sector framework, both $k[t]$ as well as $h[t]$ can be accumulated, an assumption that splits the planner's problem in 7)-11) into two separate decisions: a technological decision on which factor to accumulate, (that characterizes the transitional dynamics of the system); and a consumption-

---

[6] The speed of convergence $\beta[d^*]$ is, in fact, the speed at which the physical to human capital ratio, $d[t]$, as well as the rate of growth of consumption $\gamma_c[d[t]]$, locally converge to their steady-state equilibrium. As shown in Appendix 2, two possibilities may arise for the convergence of the rates of growth of $k[t]$ and $h[t]$, $\gamma_k[.]$ and $\gamma_h[.]$. For the case in which the steady-state physical to human capital intensitivity used in the production of total output is higher than that used in the production of human capital, then $\gamma_k[.]$ and $\gamma_h[.]$ also converge at the speed $\beta[d^*]$. On the other hand, whenever factor intensitivities are reversed, $\gamma_k[.]$ and $\gamma_h[.]$ will converge at a different speed than $\beta[d^*]$, which, however, is still independent of preference parameters. In fact, in this case, $d[t]$ and $\gamma_c[d[t]]$ will reach their steady-state equilibrium before $\gamma_k[.]$ and $\gamma_h[.]$ reach theirs. See Proposition 7 in Appendix 2 for further clarification.

accumulation decision similar to the one in the Solow-Ramsey model, (that characterizes the steady-state dynamics).

The intuition for such a strong separation between the transition and steady-state dynamics of the two-sector model is the following. For as long as the marginal products $F_1[.,.]$ and $G_2[.,.]$ are not equalized, the central planner will shift resources between accumulating physical and human capital so as to benefit the most from the highest return. This is an entirely technological decision, represented by the first-order conditions 12) and 13), which does not depend on preference parameters. After a while, and under the conditions specified in Proposition A.4.3 in Appendix 4, the returns $F_1[.,.]$ and $G_2[.,.]$ are eventually equalized. From this point on, the central planner proceeds as in the Solow-Ramsey model[7], measuring the total return to accumulating physical capital against the cost of postponing consumption, so as to decide how much consumption to postpone for the future. This consumption-accumulation decision, represented by equations 4), 5), 8), 9), 10), 11), 14), will be a function of preference parameters such as $\theta[.]$ and ρ, for the reasons already explained in Section 2.2[8]. Moreover, since at this point $F_1[.,.] = G_2[.,.]$, the marginal product of physical capital is constant, the planner's consumption-accumulation decision remain unaltered and a steady-state is reached.

Also notice from equation 15) that the speed of convergence $\beta[d^*]$ is a positive function of the second derivatives $F_{11}[.,.]$ and $G_{21}[.,.]$. Thus the larger are the elasticities of the marginal products $F_1[.,.]$ and $G_2[.,.]$ to a change in the physical to human capital ratio $d[t]$, the faster $F_1[.,.]$ and $G_2[.,.]$ will converge to each other, and the more rapidly the two-sector the economy will reach its steady-state equilibrium.

2.4 Conclusion

Contrary to what happens in the Solow-Ramsey one-sector growth model, the speed of convergence of the two-sector economy is independent of preference parameters. This result is a direct consequence of the assumption that both factors of production can be accumulated. Under these circumstances, the

---

[7] The difference between the consumption-accumulation decision of the Solow-Ramsey and two-sector models lie in the fact that, in the Solow-Ramsey framework, the planner will adjust his decision until the marginal product $F_1[.,.]$ equals the discount rate; whereas in the two-sector framework his decision will remain unaltered at $F_1[.,.] = G_2[.,.]$.

[8] In order to generate steady-state growth, one needs to assume that the elasticity of intertemporal substitution in consumption $\theta[.]$ is constant. See Proposition 4 in Appendix 2.

transitional dynamics is characterized by the return to accumulating physical capital being measured against the return to accumulating human capital, rather than the cost of postponing consumption. Consequently, technological parameters that affect how fast returns are equalized, will be the sole determinants of the speed at which the two-sector economy converges towards its steady-state equilibrium.

Chapter 3

A One-Dimensional Interpretation for the Transitional Dynamics of Two-Sector Models of Endogenous Growth

By focusing on returns rather than ratios, the four dimensional non-linear differencial system that governs the dynamics of the two-sector economy is reduced to a single dimension. This implies that the only force driving the two-sector economy towards its steady-state equilibrium is returns equalization, rather than the consumption-saving decision of the Sollow-Ramsey model.

3.1 Introduction

Even though the transitional dynamics of the two-sector growth model has been the subject of intensive research, a proper account of the major force driving the economy towards its long-run equilibrium has yet to be provided. Mulligan and Sala-i-Martin (1992) was the first attempt in this direction. Their intuition was that, since consumption as well as physical and human capital eventually end up growing at a common rate, one could concentrate the analysis on how ratios, rather than levels, converged to the steady state. By looking at the dynamics from this "ratios" perspective, they were able to reduce a complicated four-dimensional non-linear differential system into three dimensions, in addition to providing some economic intuition for what they called "imbalance effects".

This chapter is in the spirit of Mulligan and Sala-i-Martin (1992), in the sense that it also simplifies the dynamics of the two-sector model with the objective of deriving some economic intuition for how the system behaves during the transition. However, by concentrating on returns rather than ratios, the transitional dynamics is reduced to a single dimension, and a clear account is provided for the one single force that drives the economy towards its long-run equilibrium, namely a tendency for returns to be equalized.

The analysis will be organized as follows. Section 3.2 states the model and derives the first-order necessary conditions for the planner's problem. Section 3.3 describes Mulligan and Sala-i-Martin (1992) three-dimensional approach and shows how it already suggested that a further reduction of the two-sector dynamics was possible. Section 3.4 concentrates the analysis on the returns to accumulating physical and human capital and shows how the transitional dynamics of the two-sector model can be reduced to a single non-linear differential equation. Section 3.5 concludes.

3.2 The Standard Two-Sector Growth Model

Consider the traditional two-sector growth model analyzed by Lucas (1988) and Barro and Sala-i-Martin (1995), where a central planner maximizes an intertemporal utility function subject to a dynamic budget constraint and a human capital accumulation condition. The control variables are per-capita consumption $c[t]$ and the fraction $u[t]$ of human capital allocated to producing the consumption good, whereas the state variables are the stocks of physical and human capital, $k[t]$ and $h[t]$. The positive discount rate is denoted by ρ, and both the consumption good as well as physical-capital are produced with the same technology. The central planner's dynamic optimization problem is described by expressions 1)-3) below:

$$1)\ Max \int_0^\infty u[c[t]] e^{-\rho t} dt$$

$$2)\ k'[t] = F[k[t], u[t]h[t]] - c[t]$$

$$3)\ h'[t] = (1 - u[t]) h[t]$$

The production function $F[.\,,.]$ is homogeneous of the first degree in $k[t]$ and $u[t].h[t]$, with positive first-order derivatives $F_1[.,.]$ and $F_2[.,.]$ and negative second-order direct derivatives $F_{11}[.,.]$ and $F_{22}[.,.]$; whereas the instantaneous utility function $u[c[t]]$ is assumed to be strictly concave in $c[t]$. Both the production function $F[.\,,.]$ as well as the instantaneous utility function $u[c[t]]$ satisfy the Inada (1963) conditions.

The first-order conditions for the planner's problem are given by:

$$4)\ c'[t] = c[t] \frac{1}{\theta[c[t]]} (F_1[k[t], u[t]h[t]] - \rho), \quad \theta[c[t]] = -\frac{c[t] u''[c[t]]}{u'[c[t]]}$$

$$5) - \frac{\partial F_2[k[t], u[t]h[t]]}{\partial t} = (F_2[k[t], u[t]h[t]])^2 (B - F_1[k[t], u[t]h[t]])$$

$$6)\ \lim_{t \to \infty} \left(\frac{k'[t]}{k[t]} - F_1[k[t], u[t]h[t]] \right) < 0$$

$$7)\ \lim_{t \to \infty} \left(\frac{h'[t]}{h[t]} - B \right) < 0$$

Equation 4) is the traditional dynamic Euler condition, stating that whenever the return to accumulating physical capital is above (below) the rate of time preference, consumption will be shifted towards the future (present) at a rate which is a positive linear function of the elasticity of intertemporal substitution $1/\theta$ $[c[t]]$. Equation 5) deals with the dynamic allocation of human capital between producing the consumption good and human capital. It states that, whenever the marginal benefit of accumulating human capital is above (below) that of accumulating physical capital, it must be the case that the opportunity cost of accumulating human capital is increasing (decreasing). Equations 6) and 7) are the usual transversality conditions. They state that if the boundary values of $k[t]$ and $h[t]$ are to be zero, the asymptotic rates at which physical and human capital are accumulated must be smaller than the asymptotic returns.

If we rewrite equation 5) in terms of $u'[t]$, we get that:

$$5') \; u'[t] = u[t] \frac{k[t]}{h[t]} \left(\frac{k'[t]}{k[t]} - \frac{h'[t]}{h'[t]} \right) + u[t]^2 \frac{h[t]}{k[t]} \frac{F_2[k[t], u[t]h[t]]^2}{F_{21}[k[t], u[t]h[t]]} \left(B - F_1[k[t], u[t]h[t]] \right)$$

Equations 2), 3), 4) and 5') form a four dimensional non-linear system of differential equations in $k[t]$, $h[t]$, $c[t]$ and $u[t]$ which, together with the transversality conditions, completely characterizes the dynamic behavior of the two-sector economy. In particular, it can be shown that, whenever the instantaneous utility function in 1) takes a constant elasticity of intertemporal substitution form, the economy will locally converge to a resting state in which $c[t]$, $k[t]$ and $h[t]$ all grow at a common constant rate γ^*, whereas $u[t]$ is constant[1]. However, the analysis of the transitional dynamics of this four-dimensional dynamic system is difficult to solve and gives little economic intuition for the forces that come into play in bringing $c[t]$, $k[t]$, $h[t]$ and $u[t]$ to their long-run equilibrium.

3.3 The Three Dimensional Approach of Mulligan and Sala-i-Martin

Mulligan and Sala-i-Martin (1992) considerably simplified the transitional dynamics of the two-sector model by looking at it from an "imbalance" perspective, in which "the growth rate .... is higher the larger is the magnitude of the gap between the ratio of physical to human capital and the steady-state value of this ratio"[2]. Their main intuition was that, since $c[t]$, $k[t]$ and $h[t]$ will eventually grow at a common rate γ^*, one should take a closer look at ratios rather than levels, and then interpret the transitional dynamics in terms of how $\Psi[t] = k[t]/h[t]$, $\chi[t] = c[t]/k[t]$ as well as $u[t]$ converge to their constant steady-state values[3] Ψ^*, χ^* and u^*.

---

[1] See Caballé and Santos (1992) for further clarification on the transitional dynamics and stability properties of the two-sector growth model.
[2] Barro and Sala-i-Martin (1995), page 172.
[3] The "imbalance" interpretation of Mulligan and Sala-i-Martin is more general than the "returns" interpretation of Section 3.4. In particular, in the presence of externalities, it can still reduce the four-dimension non-linear differential system in equations 2), 3), 4), 5'), to three dimensions, whereas the "returns" interpretation will not be of any help in this case.

This "imbalance" interpretation allowed for the reduction of the four-dimensional non-linear system in 2)-5'), into a three dimensional system in $\Psi[t]$, $\chi[t]$, and $u[t]$, given by equations 8)-10) below:

$$8)\ \psi'[t] = u[t] f\left[\frac{\psi[t]}{u[t]}, 1\right] - \chi[t].\psi[t] - \psi[t] B(1 - u[t])$$

$$9)\ u'[t] = \frac{u[t]}{\psi[t]} \psi'[t] - \frac{u[t]}{\psi[t]} g\left[\frac{\psi[t]}{u[t]}\right]$$

$$10)\ \chi'[t] = \chi[t] \left\{ \frac{1}{\theta}\left(F_1\left[\frac{\psi[t]}{u[t]}, 1\right] - \rho \right) - \frac{\psi'[t]}{\psi[t]} + B(1 - u[t]) \right\}$$

Notice that it was assumed that the elasticity of intertemporal substitution in consumption $\theta[c[t]] = \theta$ was constant, when writing equation 10). The function $g[\psi[t]/u[t]]$ is a measure of the difference between the marginal product of accumulating human capital and the marginal product of accumulating physical capital, and is given by equation 11):

$$11)\ g\left[\frac{\psi[t]}{u[t]}\right] = \frac{F_2\left[\frac{\psi[t]}{u[t]}, 1\right]^2}{F_{21}\left[\frac{\psi[t]}{u[t]}, 1\right]} \left(B - F_1\left[\frac{\psi[t]}{u[t]}, 1\right] \right)$$

By taking a Taylor expansion of the differential system in 8)-10) around its steady-state equilibrium $\psi'[t] = 0$, $\chi'[t] = 0$, $u'[t] = 0$ one is able to get that:

$$12)\ \begin{bmatrix} \psi^*{}'[t] \\ u^*{}'[t] \\ \chi^*{}'[t] \end{bmatrix} = \begin{bmatrix} J_{11}^* & -\frac{\psi^*}{u^*}J_{11}^* + \psi^* B & \psi^* \\ \frac{u^*}{\psi^*}J_{11}^* - \frac{u^*}{\psi^*}g'\left[\frac{\psi^*}{u^*}\right] & -J_{11}^* + u^* B + g'\left[\frac{\psi^*}{u^*}\right] & -u^* \\ J_{31}^* & -\frac{\psi^*}{u^*}J_{31}^* & \chi^* \end{bmatrix} \begin{bmatrix} \psi^*[t] \\ u^*[t] \\ \chi^*[t] \end{bmatrix}$$

where the terms with a star superscript "*" indicate steady-state values, and the exact expressions for the J_{ij}^* terms of the Jacobian Matrix J^* are calculated in Appendix 5.

The dynamic system in 12) can be proven to be locally saddle-path stable, with roots given by:

$$13)\ \lambda^* = g'\left[\frac{\psi^*}{u^*}\right] < 0$$

$$14)\ \lambda_1^* = \chi^* > 0$$

$$15)\ \lambda_2^* = Bu^* > 0$$

Notice that, contrary to what happens in the one-sector growth model, the stable root λ^* does not depend on utility parameters such as θ and ρ. This feature, which was recently noted by Ortigueira and Santos (1997) and Tenani (1997), has to do with the fact that the first two-rows of the characteristic matrix of the dynamic system in 12) will be linearly dependent whenever $\lambda^* = g'[\psi^*/u^*]$.[4] That is, the $\chi^* = c^*/k^*$ line will not affect the determination of the stable local dynamics of the two-sector economy.

3.4 A One-Dimensional Interpretation

The fact that the stable local dynamics of the two-sector model is completely determined by the $\psi'[t]$ and $u'[t]$ equations suggests that Mulligan and Sala-i-Martin (1992)'s simplification could be taken one step further. In particular, if one defines the variable $d[t] = k[t]/(u[t].h[t])$ to be the fraction of physical to human capital used in the production of the consumption good, equation 5) can be rewritten as:

$$5")\ d'[t] = g[[d[t]]]$$

So that the dynamics of $d[t]$ is completely determined by equation 5''), being independent of equations 2)-4)[5]. Moreover, since the derivative $g'[d[t]] = \lambda$ is negative when evaluated at $d'[t] = 0$, it must be the case that $d[t]$ will locally converge to its steady-state value d^*, no matter what the central planner's decisions on $k[t]$, $h[t]$ and $c[t]$ are.

The intuition for the striking separation between the dynamics of $d[t]$ and those of $k[t]$, $h[t]$ and $c[t]$ has to do with the fact that, independently of preferences, the central planner's maximizing behavior ultimately imply that resources will be allocated to accumulating whatever "asset" yields the highest return. In this sense, whenever $F_1[d[t]]$ is greater (smaller) than B, and the return to accumulating physical capital is above (below) that of accumulating human

---

4 I thank Kelvin Lancaster for pointing this out.
5 This fact was pointed out by Barro and Sala-i-Martin (1995).

capital, resources will be shifted to accumulating physical (human) capital. This fact, together with the assumption of decreasing marginal products, imply that $F_I[d[t]]$ will be falling (increasing) until returns are equalized and the central planner's decisions remain unaltered.

Using the definition of $d[t]$ to substitute for $k[t]/(u[t].h[t])$ and $u[t]$ in equations 2)-4) yields[6]:

$$16) \begin{bmatrix} k'[t] \\ h'[t] \\ c'[t] \end{bmatrix} = \begin{bmatrix} A_{11}[d[t]] & 0 & -1 \\ A_{21}[d[t]] & B & 0 \\ 0 & 0 & A_{31}[d[t]] \end{bmatrix} \begin{bmatrix} k[t] \\ h[t] \\ c[t] \end{bmatrix}$$

where the exact expressions for the $A_{ij}[d[t]]$ terms are given in Appendix 6.

Thas is, what at first seemed to be a non-linear three-dimensional system of differential equations in $k[t]$, $h[t]$ and $c[t]$, is actually a linear non-autonomous system[7], indicating that the central planner's savings, human capital and consumption decisions will be adjusting to the dynamics of $d[t]$. In other words, there is a tendency for returns to be equalized, and everything else adjusts to it.

Once returns are equalized, a steady state is reached and it is possible to show that $k^*[t]$, $h^*[t]$, $c^*[t]$ will be growing at a constant rate γ^*, whereas u^* will be constant. To do this notice that, for $d[t] = d^*$, the solution to the linear system in 16) is given by:

$$17)\ k^*[t] = \Psi_0.e^{\gamma[d^*].t} + \Psi_1.e^{\gamma_1[d^*].t} + \Psi_2.e^{\gamma_2[d^*].t}$$

$$18)\ h^*[t] = \Psi_0.x_2[d^*].e^{\gamma[d^*].t} + \Psi_1.v_2[d^*].e^{\gamma_1[d^*].t} + \Psi_2.m_2.e^{\gamma[d^*].t}$$

$$19)\ c^*[t] = \Psi_0.x_3[d^*].e^{\gamma[d^*].t}$$

where Ψ_1, Ψ_2 and Ψ_3 are arbitrary constants; $\gamma[d^*]$, $\gamma_1[d^*]$, $\gamma_2[d^*]$ are the eigenvalues of the matrix in 16); and $x_i[d^*]$, $v_i[d^*]$, $m_i[d^*]$ are, respectively, the ith element of the eigenvectors correspondent to the $\gamma[d^*]$, $\gamma_1[d^*]$, $\gamma_2[d^*]$ eigenvalues[8]; all being evaluated at $d[t] = d^*$.

---

[6] I thank Pedro Paulo Schirmer for suggesting this transformation.
[7] The result that the three dimensional system in 16) is linear, requires the elasticity of intertemporal substitution in consumption to be constant.
[8] The closed form expressions for $\gamma[d^*]$, $\gamma_1[d^*]$, $\gamma_2[d^*]$, $x_i[d^*]$, $v_i[d^*]$, $m_i[d^*]$ are derived in Appendix 2. Notice that, when writing equation 19), it was already taken into account that $v3[d^*] = m3[d^*] = 0$.

However, not all the solutions specified in 17)-19) will satisfy the optimality conditions in equations 4)-7). To rule out these solutions note that, from Appendix 6, the eigenvalues $\gamma_1[d^*]$ and $\gamma_2[d^*]$ are both positive. Therefore, if the arbitrary constants Ψ_2 and Ψ_3 are different than zero, the central planner will end up accumulating physical capital at a different rate than the rate at which consumption is increased. Two possibilities may arise: i) if $k^{*'}[t]/k^*[t] < c^{*'}[t]/c^*[t]$, then $c^*[t]/k^*[t] \to \infty$ and, from equation 2), $k^{*'}[t]/k^*[t] \to -\infty$. Thus, after a while, $k[t] = 0$ and none of the consumption good will be produced. At this point, the central planner has to abruptly reduce consumption and the dynamic Euler equation in 4) is violated; ii) if $k^{*'}[t]/k^*[t] > c^{*'}[t]/c^*[t]$, then $c^*[t]/k^*[t] \to 0$ and, from equation 2), $k^{*'}[t]/^*[t] = F[d^*, 1]/d$ which is a rate of physical capital accumulation above $F_1[d^*, 1]$, so that the transversality condition in 2.8) is violated.

On account that possibilities i) and ii) violate either the dynamic Euler equation or the transversality condition, it must be the case that $k^{*'}[t]/k^*[t] = c^{*'}[t]/c^*[t]$ and, from 17)-19) $\Psi_1 = \Psi_2 = 0$[9]. Substituting $\Psi_1 = \Psi_2 = 0$ into 17)-19) it is possible to derive the exact form of those solutions to 16) which will satisfy the optimality conditions for the planner's problem:

17') $k^*[t] = \Psi_0 . e^{\gamma[d^*].t}$

18') $h^*[t] = \Psi_0 \left\{ \dfrac{A_{21}[d^*]}{\left(A_{22}[d^*] - \gamma^*[d^*]\right)} \right\} . e^{\gamma[d^*].t}$

19') $c^*[t] = \Psi_0 \left\{ \left(A_{11}[d^*] - \gamma[d^*]\right) - \dfrac{A_{12}[d^*] A_{21}[d^*]}{\left(A_{22}[d^*] - \gamma[d^*]\right)} \right\} . e^{\gamma[d^*].t}$

where the expressions for $x_i[d^*]$ were substituted from Appendix 6 and the common rate of growth of $k[t]$, $h[t]$ and $c[t]$ is given by:

20) $\gamma^* = \dfrac{1}{\theta}(B - \rho)$

---

[9] Notice that, up to this point, the argument does not depend on the elasticity of intertemporal substitution in consumption being constant. That is, it is always true that $d[t] \to d^*$, and $k'[t]/k[t] = h'[t]/h[t] = c'[t]/c[t]$. In fact, the constant elasticity of substitution assumption will solely imply that the common growth rate, $\gamma[t] = (F_1[d^*, 1] - \delta_k - \rho)/\theta$, is also constant.

Moreover, since at the steady-state equilibrium $d[t] = d^*$ and $k^{*'}[t]/k^*[t] = h^{*'}[t]/h^*[t]$, then, by the definition of $d[t]$, it must be the case that $u[t] = u^*$.

3.5 Conclusion

This chapter provides a one-dimensional interpretation of the transitional dynamics of the two-sector growth model. By focusing on the fact that the central planner will allocate resources in accumulating the factor which yields the highest return, it was shown that the transitional dynamics of the two-sector economy is also implicit in the behavior of the fraction $d[t]$ of physical to human capital used in the production of the consumption good. The consumption as well as the physical and human capital dynamics will then adjust to $d[t]$ in a linear but non-autonomous fashion.

Appendixes

Appendix 1: The Intertemporal Allocation Condition

For the general case in which $G_1 \neq 0$ and $G_2 \neq 0$, as well as for the particular cases in which $G_2 = 0$ and $G_1 = 0$, equation 18) in chapter 1 can be rewritten as:

$$A.1.1)\, d'[t] = \left\{ \frac{\left(F_1[d[t],\,1]-\delta_k\right) - \left(G_1\left[E\left[\frac{w[d[t]]}{P_b}\right],\,1\right]-\delta_h\right)}{\eta_{F_2,d}[d[t]]\left(1-\eta_{G_1,E}\left[\frac{w[d[t]]}{P_b}\right]\eta_{E,w/P_b}\left[\frac{w[d[t]]}{P_b}\right]\right)} \right\} d[t], \text{ for } G_1 \neq 0, G_2 \neq 0$$

$$A.1.2)\, d'[t] = \left\{ \frac{\left(F_1[d[t],\,1]-\delta_k\right) - \left(G_1-\delta_h\right)}{\eta_{F_2,d}[d[t]]} \right\} d[t], \text{ for } G_2 = 0$$

$$A.1.3)\, F_1[d[t],\,1] - \delta_k = \frac{F_2[d[t],\,1]}{P_b} G_2 - \delta_h, \text{ for } G_1 = 0$$

$$A.1.4)\, \eta_{F_2,d}[d[t]] = F_{2,1}[d[t],\,1]\frac{d[t]}{F_2[d[t],\,1]} > 0$$

$$A.1.5)\, \eta_{G_1,E}[d[t]] = -G_{11}\left[E\left[\frac{w[d[t]]}{P_b}\right],\,1\right]\frac{E\left[\frac{w[d[t]]}{P_b}\right]}{G_1\left[E\left[\frac{w[d[t]]}{P_b}\right],\,1\right]} > 0$$

$$A.1.6)\, \eta_{E,w/P_b}[d[t]] = -\frac{1}{\eta_{G_1,E}[d[t]]\left(1+\frac{F_2[d[t]]}{P_b}E\left[\frac{w[d[t]]}{P_b}\right]\right)} > 0$$

where the elasticities $\eta_{F_2,d}[d[t]]$, $\eta_{G_1,E}[w[t]/P_b]$ and $\eta_{E,w/P_b}[w[t]/P_b]$ are given by:

Notice that the elasticity in A.1.6) implies that the denominator of A1.1) is positive.

Appendix 2: The Non-Autonomous System in k[t], h[t] and c[t]

For the "general schooling" production function ($G_1 \neq 0$ and $G_2 \neq 0$) the matrix terms A_{ij} in equation 19) in chapter 1 are as follows:

$$\text{A.2.1)} \, A_{11}[d[t]] = \frac{F_2[d[t], 1]}{d[t]} + (F_1[d[t], 1] - \delta_k - n) + \frac{P_b}{E\left[\frac{w[d[t]]}{P_b}\right] d[t]} > 0$$

$$\text{A.2.2)} \, A_{12}[d[t]] = \frac{P_b}{E\left[\frac{w[d[t]]}{P_b}\right]} > 0$$

$$\text{A.2.3)} \, A_{21}[d[t]] = \frac{B\left[\frac{w[d[t]]}{P_b}\right]}{d[t]} > 0$$

$$\text{A.2.4)} \, A_{22}[d[t]] = B\left[\frac{w[d[t]]}{P_b}\right] - (\delta_h - n)$$

$$\text{A.2.5)} \, A_{33}[d[t]] = \frac{1}{\theta}(F_1[d[t], 1] - \delta_k - n)$$

The "public library" case can be derived from the above expressions by setting $G_2 = 0$, which implies that $B[.] = G_1$, $b[t] = 0$, and thus $E[.] \to \infty$.

The eigenvalues of the matrix in 19) are given by:

$$\text{A.2.6)} \, \gamma[d[t]] = \frac{1}{\theta}(F_1[d[t], 1] - \delta_k - n)$$

$$\text{A.2.7)} \, \gamma_1[d[t]] = \frac{(A_{11}[.] + A_{22}[.]) + \sqrt{(A_{11}[.] + A_{22}[.])^2 - 4(A_{11}[.]A_{22}[.] - A_{12}[.]A_{21}[.])}}{2}$$

$$\text{A.2.8)} \, \gamma_2[d[t]] = \frac{(A_{11}[.] + A_{22}[.]) - \sqrt{(A_{11}[.] + A_{22}[.])^2 - 4(A_{11}[.]A_{22}[.] - A_{12}[.]A_{21}[.])}}{2}$$

One needs to determine the signs of $\gamma_1[d^*]$ and $\gamma_2[d^*]$. To do this, notice that, for the "general schooling" production function ($G_1 \neq 0$ and $G_2 \neq 0$), the average product of that fraction of human capital allocated to studying can be calculated to be:

$$\text{A.2.9)} \ B\left[E\left[\frac{w[d^*]}{P_b}\right]\right] = G_1\left[E\left[\frac{w[d^*]}{P_b}\right], 1\right] \frac{1}{w[d^*]/P_b} \frac{1}{E\left[w[d^*]/P_b\right]} \left(1 + \frac{w[d^*]}{P_b} \frac{w[d^*]}{P_b}\right)$$

If we substitute $B[E[w[d^*]/P_b]$, as well as the steady-state value of $G_1[d^*, .] = r[d^*] + \delta_h$ into A.24) we get that, at the steady-state:

$$\text{A.2.10)} \ A_{22}\left[d^*\right] = \frac{(r[d^*] + \delta_h)}{w[d^*]/P_b} \frac{1}{E\left[w[d^*]/P_b\right]} + (r[d^*] - n) > 0$$

where, it was taken into account that $r[d^*] > n$, so that the transversality condition in 8) is satisfied for positive $a'[t]/a[t]$[1].

One needs to calculate the sign of $A_{11}[d^*] A_{22}[d^*] - A_{12}[d^*] A_{21}[d^*]$. Using equations A.2.1)-A2.4), A.2.9) as well as the fact that, at the steady-state, $G_1[d^*, .] = r[d^*] + \delta_h$, yields:

$$\text{A.2.11)} \ A_{11}\left[d^*\right]A_{22}\left[d^*\right] + A_{12}\left[d^*\right]A_{21}\left[d^*\right] = \left(\frac{w[d^*]}{d^*} + (r[d^*] - n)\right) A_{22}\left[d^*\right] > 0$$

where, once again, it was taken into account that $r[d^*] > n$.

Equations A.2.10) and A.2.11) imply that the eigenvalues $\gamma_1[d[t]]$ and $\gamma_2[d[t]]$, in equations A.2.7) and A.2.8), when evaluated at $d[t] = d^*$, will have positive real parts.

Finally, the eigenvector correspondent to $\gamma[d[t]]$, with the first element normalized to one, is given by:

$$\text{A.2.12)} \begin{bmatrix} x_1 \\ x_2 \\ x_3 \end{bmatrix} = \begin{bmatrix} 1 \\ A_{21}[d[t]]/(A_{22}[d[t]] - A_{33}[d[t]]) \\ (A_{11}[d[t]] - A_{33}[d[t]]) - (A_{12}[d[t]]A_{21}[d[t]])/(A_{22}[d[t]] - A_{33}[d[t]]) \end{bmatrix}$$

---

[1] If $r[d^*] < n$, the transversality condition will only be satisfied for negative $a'[t]/a[t]$. We can rule out the case of negative $a'[t]/a[t]$, however, by an argument similar to the one used in Proposition 2 in chapter 1.

Appendix 3: The Solow-Ramsey Model

Propositions A.3.1 and A.3.2 below illustrates how the assumption of decreasing marginal products, together with the Inada conditions and the hypothesis that physical capital is the only factor being accumulated, will ultimately imply that the Ramsey-Solow economy locally converges to a zero growth equilibrium.

Proposition A.3.1: *In the Solow-Ramsey one-sector growth model, the steady-state equilibrium is characterized by constant levels of consumption and physical capital.*

Proof: Denote the steady-state growth rates of consumption and physical capital by γ_c^* and γ_k^*. To prove that the steady-state levels of $k[t]$ and $c[t]$ are constants, first notice that γ_c^* and γ_k^* cannot be negative, since the non-negativity constraints in equation 3) would eventually be violated. Moreover, by taking the limit of equation 2) as time goes to infinity, one can use L'Hopital rule as well as the assumption that $F[.,.]$ is homogeneous of degree one to get that:

$$A.1.1) \; \gamma_k^* = \lim_{t \to \infty} \gamma_k^* = \lim_{t \to \infty} F_1\left[\frac{k[t]}{h}, 1\right] - \lim_{t \to \infty} \frac{c[t]}{k[t]}$$

If γ_k^* is positive, then the assumptions that h is constant and that the Inada conditions are satisfied will imply that $F_1[.,.] = 0$ and, by A.1.1), that $\gamma_k^* \leq 0$, which is a contradiction. Since γ_k^* can be neither negative nor positive, it must be the case that it equals zero, so that the steady-state stock of physical capital, k^*, is constant.

By substituting $\gamma_k^* = 0$ into equation 2) one gets that, at the steady-state, the totality of output $F[k^*, h]$ will be consumed and the steady-state level of consumption, c^*, is a constant given by:

$$A.1.2) \; c^* = F\left[k^*, h\right]$$

Finally, substituting $\gamma_c^* = 0$ into the dynamic Euler condition in equation 4) in chapter 2, one is able to derive that the steady-state marginal product of physical capital equals the rate of time preference:

$$A.1.3) \; F_1\left[k^*, h\right] = \rho$$

Proposition A.3.2: *The steady-state equilibrium (c^*, k^*) of the Solow-Ramsey model is locally saddle-path stable.*

Proof: By taking a Taylor expansion of the non-linear differential system in equations 2) and 4) in chapter 2, around the steady-state equilibrium (c^*, k^*) given by equations A.1.2) and A.1.3), one gets that:

$$A.1.4)\begin{bmatrix} k'[t] \\ c'[t] \end{bmatrix} = \begin{bmatrix} -1 & F_1\left[k^*,h\right] \\ 0 & \dfrac{c^*}{\theta\left[c^*\right]}F_{11}\left[k^*,h\right] \end{bmatrix}\begin{bmatrix} k[t]-k^* \\ c[t]-c^* \end{bmatrix}$$

If one defines the capital share of output, $\varpi_k[.,.]$, and the elasticity of the marginal product of physical capital with respect to $k[t]$, $\eta_{F,k}[.,.]$, by:

$$A.1.5)\ \omega_k\left[k[t],h\right] = F_1\left[k[t],h[t]\right]\frac{k[t]}{F\left[k[t],h[t]\right]} > 0$$

$$A.1.6)\ \eta_{F_1,k}\left[k[t],h\right] = -F_{11}\left[k[t],h[t]\right]\frac{k[t]}{F_1\left[k[t],h[t]\right]} > 0$$

Then, the roots of the dynamic system in A.1.4) can be expressed by equations A.1.7) and A.1.8) below:

$$A.1.7)\ \lambda_s = \frac{1}{2}F_1\left[k^*,h\right]\left\{1 - \sqrt{1 + 4\frac{1}{\theta\left[c^*\right]}\frac{\eta_{F_1,k}\left[k^*,h\right]}{\omega_k\left[k^*,h\right]}}\right\} < 0$$

$$A.1.8)\ \lambda_u = \frac{1}{2}F_1\left[k^*,h\right]\left\{1 + \sqrt{1 + 4\frac{1}{\theta\left[c^*\right]}\frac{\eta_{F_1,k}\left[k^*,h\right]}{\omega_k\left[k^*,h\right]}}\right\} > 0$$

And since one root is positive and the other negative, the local dynamics of $c[t]$ and $k[t]$ around the steady-state equilibrium c^* and k^* is locally saddle-path stable.

Appendix 4: The Two-Sector Model

Propositions A.4.1-A.4.4 below deals with the transitional and steady-state dynamics of the two-sector growth model.

Proposition A.4.1: *The assumptions that F[.,.] and G[.,.] are homogeneous of degree greater than zero with positive first-order derivatives and negative second-order direct derivatives imply that, throughout the optimal path, the ratio $(1-\eta[t])k[t]/((1-u[t])h[t])$ is a positive function of the ratio $\eta[t]k[t]/(u[t]h[t])$.*

Proof: Consider the case in which $F[.,.]$ is homogeneous of the rth degree and $G[.,.]$ is homogeneous of the pth degree, with r and p greater than zero. From the traditional properties of homogeneous functions, the first-order derivatives $F_1[.,.]$ and $F_2[.,.]$ will be homogeneous of the $(r-1)^{th}$ degree, whereas the first-order derivatives $G_1[.,.]$ and $G_2[.,.]$ will be homogeneous of the $(p-1)^{th}$ degree. Equation 12) in chapter 2 can then be rewritten as:

$$A.4.1) \quad \frac{G_1\left[\frac{(1-\eta[t])k[t]}{(1-u[t])h[t]},1\right]}{G_2\left[\frac{(1-\eta[t])k[t]}{(1-u[t])h[t]},1\right]} = \frac{F_1\left[\frac{\eta[t]k[t]}{u[t]h[t]},1\right]}{F_2\left[\frac{\eta[t]k[t]}{u[t]h[t]},1\right]}$$

That is, the physical to human capital ratio used in the production of $h[t]$ is a function $E[.]$ of the physical to human capital ratio used in the production of total output:

$$A.4.2) \quad \frac{(1-\eta[t])k[t]}{(1-u[t])h[t]} = E\left[\frac{\eta[t]k[t]}{u[t]h[t]}\right]$$

To calculate the derivative of $E[.]$, totally differentiate A.4.2) to get that:

$$A.4.2) \quad \frac{(1-\eta[t])k[t]}{(1-u[t])h[t]} = E\left[\frac{\eta[t]k[t]}{u[t]h[t]}\right], \quad E'\left[\frac{\eta[t]k[t]}{u[t]h[t]}\right] > 0$$

From Euler's Theorem and the assumptions that $F[.,.]$ and $G[.,.]$ have positive first-order derivatives and negative direct second-order direct derivatives, one can derive that the cross derivatives $F_{21}[.,.]$ and $G_{21}[.,.]$ are both positive. The derivative in A.4.3) is thus positive and Equation A.4.2 can be rewritten as:

$$\text{A.4.3)} \frac{\partial\left(\frac{(1-\eta[t])k[t]}{(1-u[t])h[t]}\right)}{\partial\left(\frac{\eta[t]k[t]}{u[t]h[t]}\right)} = \frac{\left\{\frac{F_{11}[.,1]}{F_2[.,1]} - \frac{F_1[.,1]}{F_2[.,1]}F_{21}[.,1]\right\}}{\left\{\frac{G_{11}[.,1]}{G_2[.,1]} - \frac{G_1[.,1]}{G_2[.,1]}G_{21}[.,1]\right\}}$$

So that, as we wanted to prove, the ratio $(1-\eta[t])k[t]/((1-u[t])h[t])$ of physical to human capital used in the production of $h[t]$ is a positive function of the ratio $\eta[t]k[t]/(u[t]h[t])$, of physical to human capital used in the production of total output.

Proposition A.4.2: *The assumption that $F[.,.]$ and $G[.,.]$ are homogeneous of degree one and that the instantaneous utility function $U[.]$ is of the constant elasticity of substitution form, imply that the non-linear differential system in $k[t]$, $h[t]$, $c[t]$, $u[t]$ and $\eta[t]$ described by equations 4), 8), 9), 12), 13) in chapter 2 can be divided into a single first-order non-linear differential equation in $d[t] = \eta[t]k[t]/(u[t]h[t])$ and a three dimensional first-order linear system of non-autonomous differential equations in $k[t]$, $h[t]$ and $c[t]$.*

Proof: Since $F[.,.]$ and $G[.,.]$ are homogeneous of degree one, the first-order derivatives $F_1[.,.]$, $F_2[.,.]$, $G_1[.,.]$ and $G_2[.,.]$ will be homogeneous of degree zero. This fact, together with Proposition A.4.1, allows one to rewrite the first-order condition in Equation 13 in chapter 2 as:

$$\text{A.4.4)}\ d'[t] = g[d[t]]$$

Where the function $g[d[t]]$ is given by:

$$\text{A.4.5)}\ g[d[t]] = \frac{G_2[E[d[t]],1]F_2[d[t],1]}{F_2[d[t],1]G_{21}[E[d[t]],1] - G_2[E[d[t]],1]F_{21}[d[t],1]}\left(G_2[E[d[t]],1] - F_1[d[t],1]\right)$$

Equation A.4.2') as well as the definition of $d[t]$ can now be used to derive an expression for $u[t]h[t]$:

$$\text{A.4.6)}\ u[t]h[t] = \frac{k[t] - E[d[t]]h[t]}{d[t] - E[d[t]]}$$

One can then use equation A.4.2') and A.4.6), together with the assumption of linear homogeneity of $F[.,.]$ and $G[.,.]$ to rewrite equations 8) and 9) in chapter 2 as:

A.4.7) $k'[t] = \dfrac{F[d[t],1]}{d[t]-E[d[t]]} k[t] - \dfrac{F[d[t],1]}{d[t]-E[d[t]]} E[d[t]]h[t] - c[t]$

A.4.8) $h'[t] = -\dfrac{G[E[d[t]],1]}{d[t]-E[d[t]]} k[t] + \dfrac{G[E[d[t]],1]}{d[t]-E[d[t]]} d[t]h[t]$

Moreover, linear homogeneity of $F[.,.]$ and the assumption that the instantaneous utility function is of the constant elasticity of substitution form, implies that the dynamic Euler equation in 4) in chapter 2 can be rewritten as:

A.4.9) $c'[t] = c[t]\dfrac{1}{\theta}\left(F_1[d[t],1]-\rho\right)$

Thus, the non-linear differential system in equations 4), 8), 9), 12), 13) in chapter 2 can be interpreted as an autonomous non-linear differential equation in $d[t]$, represented by equation A.4.4), and a linear but non-autonomous three dimensional system in $k[t]$, $h[t]$ and $c[t]$, represented by equations A.4.7), A.4.8) and A.4.9).

Using matrix notation, one can write the dynamic system in equations A.4.7), A.4.8) and A.4.9) as:

A.4.10) $\begin{bmatrix} k'[t] \\ h'[t] \\ c'[t] \end{bmatrix} = \begin{bmatrix} A_{11}[d[t]] & A_{12}[d[t]] & -1 \\ A_{21}[d[t]] & A_{22}[d[t]] & 0 \\ 0 & 0 & A_{33}[d[t]] \end{bmatrix} \begin{bmatrix} k[t] \\ h[t] \\ c[t] \end{bmatrix}$

Where, the functions $A_{ij}[d[t]]$, $i = 1,2,3$; $j = 1,2,3$ are given by:

A.4.11) $A_{11}[d[t]] = \dfrac{F[d[t],1]}{d[t]-E[d[t]]}$

A.4.12) $A_{12}[d[t]] = -\dfrac{F[d[t],1]}{d[t]-E[d[t]]} E[d[t]]$

A.4.13) $A_{21} = -\dfrac{G[E[d[t]],1]}{d[t]-E[d[t]]}$

A.4.14) $A_{22} = \dfrac{G[E[d[t]],1]}{d[t]-E[d[t]]} d[t]$

A.4.15) $A_{33} = \dfrac{1}{\theta}\left(F_1[d[t],1]-\rho\right)$

Proposition A.4.3: *If $F[.,..]$ and $G[.,.]$ are homogeneous of degree one with positive first-order derivatives and negative second-order direct derivatives and if the steady-state elasticity of $F_1[.,..]$ with respect to $d[.]$ is greater than the steady-state elasticity of $G_2 [.,..]$ with respect to $d[.]$, then the two-sector economy will locally converge to a point at which $d[t]$ is constant at d^* and $F_1[d^*,1] = G_2 [d^*,1]$.*

Proof: Define d^* to be the point at which the marginal benefit of accumulating physical capital equals the marginal benefit of accumulating human capital so that $d'[t] = 0$:

By linearizing $d'[t]$ around d^*, one gets:

$$A.4.16)\ F_1\left[d^*,1\right] = G_2\left[E\left[d^*\right],1\right]$$

Where the speed of adjustment $\beta[\,d^*]$ is given by the following expression:

$$A.4.17)\ d'[t] = -\beta\left[d^*\right]\left(d[t]-d^*\right)$$

Notice from A.4.17) and A.4.18) that $d'[t]$ will locally converge to d^* whenever:

$$A.4.18)\beta\left[d^*\right] = -\left(\frac{G_2\left[E\left[d^*\right],1\right]F_2\left[d^*,1\right]}{F_2\left[d^*,1\right]G_{21}\left[E\left[d^*\right],1\right] - G_2\left[E\left[d^*\right],1\right]F_{21}\left[d^*,1\right]}\right)\left(G_{21}\left[E\left[d^*\right],1\right] - F_{11}\left[d^*,1\right]\right)$$

Or, as we wanted to prove:

$$A.4.19)\ F_2\left[d^*,1\right]G_{21}\left[E\left[d^*\right],1\right] < G_2\left[E\left[d^*\right],1\right]F_{21}\left[d^*,1\right]$$

$$A.4.19')\ \eta_{G_2,d}\left[d^*\right] < \eta_{F_1,d}\left[d^*\right]$$

Where the elasticities of the marginal products $G_2[.,.]$ and $F_1[.,.]$ are denoted by the following expressions:

$$A.4.20)\ \eta_{G_2,d}\left[d[t]\right] = \frac{\partial G_2\left[E\left[d[t]\right],1\right]}{\partial d[t]}\frac{d[t]}{G_2\left[E\left[d[t]\right],1\right]}$$

$$A.4.21)\ \eta_{F_1,d}\left[d[t]\right] = \frac{\partial F_1\left[d[t],1\right]}{\partial d[t]}\frac{d[t]}{F_1\left[d[t],1\right]}$$

Proposition A.4.4: *At $d[t] = d^*$, the solution for the three dimensional linear non-autonomous system in A.4.10) is of the following form:*

58 Human Capital and Growth

$$A.4.22)\, k^*[t] = \Psi_0 . e^{\gamma[d^*].t} + \Psi_1 . e^{\gamma_1[d^*].t} + \Psi_2 . e^{\gamma_2[d^*].t}$$

$$A.4.23)\, h^*[t] = \Psi_0 . x_2[d^*] . e^{\gamma[d^*].t} + \Psi_1 . v_2[d^*] . e^{\gamma_1[d^*].t} + \Psi_2 . m_2 . e^{\gamma[d^*].t}$$

$$A.4.24)\, c^*[t] = \Psi_0 . x_3[d^*] . e^{\gamma[d^*].t}$$

where Ψ_0, Ψ_1 and Ψ_2 are arbitrary constants; $\gamma[d[t]]$, $\gamma_1[d[t]]$, $\gamma_2[d[t]]$ are the eigenvalues of the matrix in A.4.10); and $x_i[d[t]]$, $v_i[d[t]]$, $m_i[d[t]]$ are, respectively, the ith element of the eigenvectors correspondent to the $\gamma[d[t]]$, $\gamma_1[d[t]]$, $\gamma_2[d[t]]$ eigenvalues; all being evaluated at $d[t] = d^*$.

Proof: At $d[t] = d^*$, the coefficients $A_{ij}[d[t]]$ in equations A.4.11)-A.4.15) are all constants, so that the three dimensional system in A.4.10) becomes a system of ordinary differential equations with constant coefficients, whose solutions are of the form stated in A.4.22-A.4.24. The eigenvalues $\gamma[d[t]]$, $\gamma_1[d[t]]$, $\gamma_2[d[t]]$ are described by equations A.4.25-A.4.27 below:

$$A.4.25)\, \gamma[d[t]] = A_{33}[.]$$

$$A.4.26)\, \gamma_1[d[t]] = \frac{(A_{11}[.] + A_{22}[.]) + \sqrt{(A_{11}[.] + A_{22}[.])^2 - 4(A_{11}[.]A_{22}[.] - A_{12}[.]A_{21}[.])}}{2}$$

$$A.4.27)\, \gamma_2[d[t]] = \frac{(A_{11}[.] + A_{22}[.]) - \sqrt{(A_{11}[.] + A_{22}[.])^2 - 4(A_{11}[.]A_{22}[.] - A_{12}[.]A_{21}[.])}}{2}$$

It is assumed that parameters are such that $A_{33}[d^*] = \gamma[d^*] \geq 0$, so that, at $d[t] = d^*$, consumption is growing at a non-negative rate. Moreover, a bit algebra reveals that whenever $d^* > E[d^*]$ and the physical to human capital ratio used in the production of total output is greater than that used in the production of human capital, then both $\gamma_1[d^*]$ and $\gamma_2[d^*]$ will be positive; whereas whenever $d^* < E[d^*]$ and the physical to human capital ratio used in the production of total output is smaller than that used in the production of human capital, then $\gamma_1[d^*]$ will be positive and $\gamma_2[d^*]$ negative.

Proposition A.4.5: *Under the assumptions of Proposition A.4.3, the two-sector economy will locally converge to a steady-state equilibrium where physical capital k[t], human capital h[t], and consumption c[t] all grow at a common constant rate $\gamma[d^*] \geq 0$.*

Proof: The first step is to show that at $t \to \infty$, physical and human capital must be growing at the same non-negative rate. This is implied by Proposition A.4.3), the human capital accumulation equation in A.4.8), the transversality condition in equation 14) in chapter 2, and the non-negativity constraint in equation 10) in chapter 2. It is then easy to show that, at $d[t] = d^*$, physical capital and consumption must also be growing at the same rate, a result which is implied by the dynamic budget constraint in A.4.7), the fact that $\gamma_k[d^*] = \gamma_h[d^*]$, the transversality condition in equation 5) in chapter 2 and the non-negativity constraint in 10) also in chapter 2. Notice that these results hold independently of whether $d^* > E[d^*]$ or $d^* < E[d^*]$.

Once it is known that as $t \to \infty$, $\gamma_k[d^*] = \gamma_h[d^*] = \gamma_c[d^*]$, one can use the results obtained about the sign of the eigenvalues in Proposition A.4.4 to show that whenever parameters are such that $d^* > E[d^*]$, then at the point at which $d[t] = d^*$, the only solutions to the dynamic system in A.4.10) which are also solutions to the planner is problem are given by:

A.4.28) $k^*[t] = \Psi_0 . e^{\gamma[d^*]t}$

A.4.29) $h^*[t] = \Psi_0 \left\{ \dfrac{A_{21}[d^*]}{\left(A_{22}[d^*] - \gamma^*[d^*]\right)} \right\} . e^{\gamma[d^*]t}$

A.4.30) $c^*[t] = \Psi_0 \left\{ \left(A_{11}[d^*] - \gamma[d^*]\right) - \dfrac{A_{12}[d^*]A_{21}[d^*]}{\left(A_{22}[d^*] - \gamma[d^*]\right)} \right\} . e^{\gamma[d^*]t}$

where we have already substituted for the eigenvectors $x_i[d^*]$.

That is, the economy reaches a balance growth path at the moment $d[t] = d^*$.

On the other hand, if parameters are such that $d^* < E[d^*]$, then, at $d[t] = d^*$, the only solutions to the dynamic system in A.4.10) which are also solutions to the planner problem are given by:

A.4.31) $k^*[t] = \Psi_0 . e^{\gamma[d^*]t} + \Psi_2 . e^{\gamma_2[d^*]t}$

A.4.32) $h^*[t] = \Psi_0 . x_2[d^*] . e^{\gamma[d^*]t} + \Psi_2 . m_2 . e^{\gamma[d^*]t}$

A.4.33) $c^*[t] = \Psi_0 . x_3[d^*] . e^{\gamma[d^*]t}$

And since in this case $\gamma_2[d^*] < 0$, the two sector economy will first reach the point at which $d[t] = d^*$ and then only asymptotically converge to a balance growth path.

Notice from equations A.4.15) and A.4.25) that, independently of whether d^* is greater or smaller than $E[d^*]$, the common balanced path rate of growth of $k[t]$, $h[t]$ and $c[t]$ is given by:

$$\text{A.4.34) } \gamma\left[d^*\right] = \frac{1}{\theta}\left(F_1\left[d^*, 1\right] - \rho\right).$$

Appendix 5: The Three Dimensional System

The Jacobian Matrix for the three dimensional system in equations 8), 9), 10) in chapter 3 is given by:

$$A.5.1) \; J = \begin{bmatrix} J_{11} & J_{12} & J_{13} \\ J_{21} & J_{22} & J_{23} \\ J_{31} & J_{32} & J_{33} \end{bmatrix}$$

Where the J_{ij}, $i = 1, 2, 3$; $j = 1, 2, 3$ terms are as follows:

$$A.5.2) \; J_{11} = \frac{\partial \psi'[t]}{\partial \psi[t]} = F_1\left[\frac{\psi[t]}{u[t]}, 1\right] - \chi[t] - B(1 - u[t])$$

$$A.5.3) \; J_{12} = \frac{\partial \psi'[t]}{\partial u[t]} = F\left[\frac{\psi[t]}{u[t]}, 1\right] - F_1\left[\frac{\psi[t]}{u[t]}, 1\right]\frac{\psi[t]}{u[t]} + \psi[t]B$$

$$A.5.4) \; J_{13} = \frac{\partial \psi'[t]}{\partial \chi[t]} = -\psi[t]$$

$$A.5.5) \; J_{21} = \frac{\partial u'[t]}{\partial \psi[t]} = \frac{u[t]}{\psi[t]}J_{11} - \psi'[t]\frac{u[t]}{\psi[t]^2} + \frac{u[t]^2}{\psi[t]^2}g\left[\frac{\psi[t]}{u[t]}\right] - \frac{u[t]}{\psi[t]}g'\left[\frac{\psi[t]}{u[t]}\right]$$

$$A.5.6) \; J_{22} = \frac{\partial u'[t]}{\partial u[t]} = \frac{u[t]}{\psi[t]}J_{12} + \psi'[t]\frac{1}{\psi[t]^2} - 2\frac{u[t]}{\psi[t]}g\left[\frac{\psi[t]}{u[t]}\right] + g'\left[\frac{\psi[t]}{u[t]}\right]$$

$$A.5.7) \; J_{23} = \frac{\partial u'[t]}{\partial \chi[t]} = \frac{u[t]}{\psi[t]}J_{13}$$

$$A.5.8) \; J_{31} = \frac{\partial \chi'[t]}{\partial \psi[t]} = \chi[t]\left\{\frac{1}{\theta}F_{11}\left[\frac{\psi[t]}{u[t]}, 1\right]\frac{1}{u[t]} + \frac{1}{\psi[t]^2}\psi'[t] - \frac{1}{\psi[t]}J_{11}\right\}$$

$$A.5.9) \; J_{32} = \frac{\partial \chi'[t]}{\partial u[t]} = \chi[t]\left\{-\frac{1}{\theta}F_{11}\left[\frac{\psi[t]}{u[t]}, 1\right]\frac{\psi[t]}{u[t]^2} - \frac{1}{\psi[t]}J_{11} + B\right\}$$

$$A.5.10) \; J_{33} = \frac{\partial \chi'[t]}{\partial \chi[t]} = \frac{1}{\theta}\left(F_1\left[\frac{\psi[t]}{u[t]}, 1\right] - \rho\right) - \frac{1}{\psi[t]}\psi'[t] - B(1 - u[t]) - \frac{\chi[t]}{\psi[t]}J_{13}$$

One want to evaluate J at the steady-state equilibrium $\Psi'[t] = u'[t] = \chi'[t] = 0$, Substituting into equations 8)-10) in chapter 3 yields:

62 Human Capital and Growth

$$\text{A.5.11) } \chi^* = \frac{u^*}{\psi^*} F\left[\frac{\psi^*}{u^*}, 1\right] - B\left(1 - u^*\right)$$

$$\text{A.5.12) } g\left(\frac{\psi^*}{u^*}\right) = 0 \rightarrow F_1\left[\frac{\psi^*}{u^*}, 1\right] = B$$

$$\text{A.5.13) } B\left(1 - u^*\right) = \frac{1}{\theta}\left(F_1\left[\frac{\psi^*}{u^*}, 1\right] - \rho\right)$$

Moreover, if one substitutes A.5.11-A.5.13) into the Jacobian Matrix in A.5.1), it will yield, after some manipulation:

$$\text{A.5.2') } J_{11}^* = -\frac{u^*}{\psi^*} F_2\left[\frac{\psi[t]}{u[t]}, 1\right]$$

$$\text{A.5.3') } J_{12}^* = J_{11}^* + \psi[t]B$$

$$\text{A.5.4') } J_{13}^* = -\psi[t]$$

$$\text{A.5.5') } J_{21}^* = \frac{u^*}{\psi^*} J_{11}^* - \frac{u^*}{\psi^*} g'\left[\frac{\psi^*}{u^*}\right]$$

$$\text{A.5.6') } J_{22}^* = \frac{u^*}{\psi^*} J_{12}^* + g'\left[\frac{\psi[t]}{u[t]}\right]$$

$$\text{A.5.7') } J_{23}^* = \frac{u^*}{\psi^*} J_{13}^*$$

$$\text{A.5.8') } J_{13}^* = \chi^*\left\{\frac{1}{\theta} F_{11}\left[\frac{\psi^*}{u^*}, 1\right] \frac{1}{u^*} - \frac{1}{\psi^*} J_{11}^*\right\}$$

$$\text{A.5.9') } J_{32}^* = -\frac{\psi^*}{u^*} J_{31}^*$$

$$\text{A.5.10') } J_{33} = \chi^*$$

To calculate the roots, first notice from equation 11) in chapter 3 that the derivative $g'[\Psi[t]/u[t]]$ will cause the first and second lines of the characteristic matrix of the Jacobian in A5.1) to be linearly dependent. Thus one can conclude that $g'[\Psi[t]/u[t]]$ is one of the roots. To derive the other two roots just factor out the third degree polynomial of the characteristic equation of J^*.

Appendix 6: The Linear Non-Autonomous System

The matrix terms A_{ij} in equation 16) in chapter 3 are as follows:

$$\text{A.6.1) } A_{11}[d[t]] = \frac{F[d[t], 1]}{d[t]} > 0$$

$$\text{A.6.2) } A_{21}[d[t]] = \frac{B}{d[t]} > 0$$

$$\text{A.6.3) } A_{33}[d[t]] = \frac{1}{\theta}\left(F_1[d[t], 1] - \delta_k - n\right)$$

The eigenvalues of the matrix in equation 19) in chapter 3 are given by the following expressions:

$$\text{A.6.4) } \gamma[d[t]] = \frac{1}{\theta}\left(F_1[d[t],1] - \rho\right)$$

$$\text{A.6.5) } \gamma_1[d[t]] = A_{11}[d[t]] > 0$$

$$\text{A.6.6) } \gamma_2[d[t]] = B > 0$$

Finally, the eigenvector correspondent to $\gamma[d[t]]$, with the first element normalized to one, is given by:

$$\text{A.6.7) } \begin{bmatrix} x_1 \\ x_2 \\ x_3 \end{bmatrix} = \begin{bmatrix} 1 \\ A_{21}[d[t]]/(A_{22}[d[t]] - A_{33}[d[t]]) \\ (A_{11}[d[t]] - A_{33}[d[t]]) \end{bmatrix}$$

REFERENCES

BARRO, Robert and Xavier Sala-i-Martin (1995): "Economic Growth". McGraw-Hill.

BENHABIB, Jess and PERLI, Roberto (1994): "Uniqueness and Indeterminacy: On the Dynamics of Endogenous Growth", *Journal of Economic Theory*, 63.

BENHABIB, Jess and SPIEGEL, Mark (1994): "The Role of Human Capital in Economic Development: Evidence from Aggregate Cross-Country Data", *Journal of Monetary Economics*, 34, pp. 143-173.

CABALLÉ, Jordi and SANTOS, Manuel (1993): "On Endogenous Growth with Physical and Human Capital", *Journal of Political Economy,* 101,6, pp.1042-1067.

INADA, Ken-Ichi (1963): "On a Two Sector Model of Economic Growth: Comments and a Generalization", *Review of Economic Studies*, 30, pp. 119-127.

LUCAS, Robert E., Jr. (1988): "On the Mechanics of Economic Development", *Journal of Monetary Economics*, 22, 1 (July), pp. 3-42.

MANKIW, N., Romer, David and WEIL, David (1992): "A Contribution to the Empirics of Economic Growth", *Quarterly Journal of Economics*, 106, pp. 407-437.

MULLIGAN, Casey B. and Sala-i-Martin, XAVIER (1993): "Transitional Dynamics in Two-Sector Models of Economic Growth". *Quarterly Journal of Economics*, 108, 3 (August), pp. 737-773.

ORTIGUEIRA, Salvaldor and SANTOS, Manuel (1997): "On the Speed of Convergence in Endogenous Growth Models". *American Economic Review,* 87,3, pp.383-399.

REBELLO, Sérgio (1991): "Long-Run Policy analysis and Long-Run Growth". *Journal of Political Economy*, 99, 3, (June) pp.500-521.

ROMER, Paul (1986): "Increasing Returns and Long-Run Growth". *American Economic Review*, 32, pp. 1002-10037.

TENANI, Paulo (1997): "Education and Growth". *Mimeo,* Columbia University, July.

UZAWA, Hirofumi (1961): "On a Two-Sector Model of Economic Growth". *Review of Economic Studies*, 78, pp. 40-47.

INDEX

A

aggregate supply, 12
aggregated demand, 12
Aldo Rustichini, VII
arbitrary constants, 19, 44
asset holdings, 6
assets, XVI, 3
asymptotic, 8, 29, 41, 59
autonomous non-linear differential equation, 56
average product, 12

B

balance growth path, 59
Benhabib, 3
boundary, 8, 29, 33, 40

C

Caballé and Santos, XV, 41
capital share, 29, 30, 53
Casey Mulligan, 3
central planner, 27
CES utility function, VII, 14, 29
characteristic equation, 62
characteristic matrix, VII, XVI, 43
Closed form expressions, 4
Cobb-Douglas, VII, 15
concave, XV, 5, 28
conditional convergence, 17
consistency conditions, 31
constant elasticity of intertemporal substitution, 28, 41
constant elasticity of substitution, 14
consumption, IX, XV, XVI, 4, 5, 7, 14, 27, 30, 44
consumption-accumulation decision, 27, 34
consumption good, 4, 5, 6
control, 9, 28, 31, 39

converge, 4
convergence, IX, XV, 15

D

Dan Biller, VII
depreciation, 6, 12
differential equation, IX, XV, 17
differential system, IX
discount rate, XVI, 5, 16, 27
Duncan Foley, VII
dynamic allocation, 11, 40
dynamic budget constraint, VII, 5, 28, 39
dynamic constraints, 7
dynamic Euler condition, 8, 19, 21, 45
dynamic Euler equation, VII
dynamic optimization, 5, 30
dynamic properties, 3
dynamic system, 41

E

economic growth, XV, 3
education, XV, XVI, 3, 4, 5, 6
effective labor, 11
efficiency condition, 32
eigenvalues, 18, 44
eigenvectors, 19, 44
elasticities, 34
elasticity, 30
elasticity of intertemporal substitution, 8, 14, 16, 20, 29
elasticity of substitution, 20
elasticity of the marginal product, 53
endogenous growth, 1
endogenous labor, 6
Euler equation, 13
Euler's Theorem, 54
expenditures, 5
externalities, 41

F

factor intensitivities, 33
factor markets, 11
factor of production, 27
factor prices, 14
factor returns, 18
feasibility constraint, 7
firms, 12, 14
first order conditions, 4, 28
first order derivatives, 6, 7, 9, 28
formal instruction, XV, 4-7, 9, 18, 23

G

general equilibrium, 1, 3, 12, 14
growth rate, 1, 5
Growth Theory, VII
growth, 3

H

Hirofumi Uzawa, 3
homogeneous functions, 54
homogeneous of the first degree, XV, 6
homogeneous, IX, 12, 28, 54
human capital, IX, XV, XVI, 1, 3, 4, 5, 6, 44
human capital accumulation condition, VII, 31, 39

I

imbalance effects, 39
Inada conditions, 5, 6, 12, 52
infinite-horizon, 28
inputs, 6
instantaneous utility function, XVI, 5, 14
interest income, 5
interest rate, 3, 7
intertemporal allocation, 10, 14
intertemporal utility function, 5, 7, 28
Investment, 1, 3, 4, 5
iso-education curves, 7

J

Jacobian Matrix, 42, 61
Jess Benhabib, VII
Jordi Caballé, 3

K

Kelvin Lancaster, VII

L

L'Hopital rule, 52
labor market, 3, 5
labor services, 5
labor-leisure choice, 6
leisure, 5, 7
library, 3, 11
linear homogeneous, VII, XVI, 4, 9, 11, 12, 28, 29, 31, 55
linear non-autonomous system, 4, 44
linearly dependent, VII, XVI, 43
local convergence, 15
local dynamics, 53
long-run dynamics, 4
long-run growth rate, 4
long-term growth, XV
Lucas model, 5
Lucas, 3

M

Mankiw, 3
Manuel Santos, 3
marginal product, 1, 3, 4, 8, 9, 10, 30
marginal rate of transformation, 8, 32
marginal return, 23
Mark Spiegel, VII, 3
market equilibrium, 14, 19
matrix, 18, 56
Mulligan and Sala-i-Martin, XV

N

night school, 5, 7, 9, 10, 17
non-autonomous differential equations, 55
non-autonomous differential system, IX

non-autonomous system, XV
non-autonomous, 14, 46
non-leisure human capital, 6, 9
non-linear differential equation, 4, 55
non-linear differential system, XV, 4, 53, 56
non-linear differential, 29
non-linear, IX
non-negativity conditions, 7, 28, 31
Non-Ponzi Game condition, 7, 19

O

one-dimensional, 46
one-sector growth model, 9
on-the-job learning, 7
opportunity cost, XVI, 3
optimal path, 11, 54
optimal solution, 32
optimality conditions, 19, 45
ordinary differential equations, 58

P

Paul Romer, XV, 3
Paulo Tenani, 13
Pedro Paulo Schirmer, VII
Perli, 3
physical capital, VII, XV, XVI, 11, 12, 30
planner's problem, 32
polynomial, 62
population, 5
population growth rate, 5
portfolio, 14, 17
preference parameters, VII, XVI, 27, 30, 32
production, 12
production function, IX, XV, XVI, 4-7, 9, 10, 17
production technology, 27
Profit maximization, 12
public library, 3, 7, 9, 10, 11
purchasing power, 10, 23

R

Ramsey Model, 9
rate of intertemporal substitution in consumption, 27

rate of time preference, 5, 8, 13, 21, 28
real interest rate, 6, 13
real resources, 6
real wage, XVI, 3, 11
relative price, 5, 8
representative consumer, 5
return, IX, 4
returns equalization, IX
Robert Lucas, XV, 3
Roberto Apelfeld, VII
Roberto Perli, VII, 3
Ron Miller, VII
roots, 42, 53

S

saddle-path, 4, 29, 42, 53
Santos and Ortigueira (1997), 13
savings, 44
school, XV, XVI, 1, 3, 11
schooling, 1, 3, 5
second order direct derivatives, 6, 28
sensitive, 30
separation, 34
Sergio Rebelo, 3
Solow-Ramsey model, 27
Solow-Ramsey one-sector growth model, 27
speed of convergence, VII, XVI, 4, 13
stability, IX
stable root, 43
state variables, 39
state, 9, 28
static allocation, 31
steady-state, IX, XVI, 1, 3, 4, 9
strictly concave, 28, 40

T

Taylor expansion, 15, 42, 53
technological, 27, 30, 33, 34
technology, 5, 11
third order derivatives, 15

three-dimensional linear non-autonomous system, VII
three-dimensional system, VII
time paths, 7
total demand, 6
total expenditure, 12
total income, 5
transition, 4
transitional dynamics, VII, XV, 1, 4, 14, 17, 27
transitional, 3
transversality condition, 8, 19
two-sector economy, IX
two-sector growth model, VII, XV, 4, 23
two-sector model, VII

U

unbounded, 5
utility function, XV
utility, VII

W

wage income, 5, 6
wage rate, 6, 7
Weil, 3
Werner Baer, VII
work, 3

X

Xavier Sala-i-Martin, VII, 3